Surviving
Middle
School

A Practical Guide For Parents

Ellen Fellenz

ISBN: 1469986477
ISBN 13: 9781469986470

Library of Congress Control Number: 2012901883
CreateSpace, North Charleston, SC

Table of Contents

Chapter 1

Introduction—
How to use this book

A fellow educator once told me that her goal was to help students thrive, not just survive. The goal of this book is to help parents do the same while their children are in middle school. Middle school offers many challenges for families. Here you will find practical, easy to implement solutions to these challenges, as well as tools to keep the connection with your child during these years. Preserving your relationship with your child is not only important to make it through the middle school years, but essential to being an effective parent during the next stage of adolescence, Teenagers. This book was written to help you retain your sanity and sense of humor while persevering through these often challenging times as a parent.

Parenting is not an easy job. So many parents have said to me, "If they (my kids) only came with a book!" Well, here is the book to get you through the tough middle-school years. By the way, only great parents read books like this. Great parents are always looking for ways to improve their parenting skills and new strategies to try out when difficult situations come up. Consider this book a way to fine-tune your already good parenting skills.

Why this book

While working as a middle-school counselor, I offered parenting classes in the evenings to help parents just like you find creative ways to tackle the challenges of middle school and the "tween" years. While creating the curriculum for the parenting courses, I found that there was very little written about this age group and specifically about middle school. The concept of middle-school education is a relatively new concept in our current education system. Middle schools have been around for about 30 years and in my opinion, are still works in progress.

The reasons for creating middle schools vary from state to state, but the issues tend to be focused on use of facilities, funding and class sizes, not the needs of children this age and what would be best for their education. In most areas, middle schools encompass sixth, seventh and eighth grades, primarily 11- to 13-year-olds. Middle schools have replaced what was formerly known as "junior high" schools that offered only seventh and eighth grades previously. But now that middle schools are here, and seem to be here to stay, there is good research being done on how best to educate young adolescents of this age group. Unfortunately, due to budget and resource constraints, much of this good research doesn't always make its way into the classrooms and programs of most middle schools. Hence, the need for books like this, and parents like you, who are willing to take the extra effort to find something that works.

Who would be crazy enough to work in a middle school?

When I began my quest to become a school counselor, I had my sights set on working in a high school. But after doing some internship work in high schools, I realized that the role of the school counselor was quite different than I had hoped. The focus was on computer schedules and modeling to make sure the right classes were being offered to the right students, etc. As a hopeful school counselor, I didn't want to work with computers and schedules; I wanted to work with kids and their families.

Further into my graduate studies, I was required to do an internship in a middle school and that was it. I knew I had found the place for me. Middle schools are far from perfect, but the children are incredible and really want guidance. They want to understand the crazy emotional and physical changes that are going on in their bodies even if they can't express it. Middle school is a time when children are still quite impressionable and with the right approach, you can have a great impact on their learning and growing into adulthood.

The bottom line is that there are many smart, talented and dedicated educators who have chosen to devote their careers to educating middle-school students. This isn't true for every teacher you are going to find in your child's middle school, but hopefully it will be the majority. Over my years working in middle schools, many educators and administrators have shared how they love the creativity and genuine nature that comes with children of this age group. They also talk about the amazement of watching middle students grow and change over these three years; emotional, physical and intellectual changes alike. I remember one school year at our first staff meeting, the teachers and staff held a contest by showing each child's sixth-grade school photo and then the staff had to guess who the children were by matching these with their eighth-grade school photos. Everyone was amazed at how much the students had changed over three short school years. Incredible.

Parents change, too

Parents face many challenges today: careers, divorce, financial struggles, safety for your children, caring for yourself, etc. And many parents tend to see getting their kids to middle school as a relief. Parents have shared with me, "My child is finally old enough to stay home alone after school" or "I don't need to volunteer at school anymore because my child is older now" or "They can do their own homework and manage their assignments themselves now" or "They don't want me around at school anymore."

Young adolescents in middle school want and need guidance, caring, supervision, attention and love even if they tell you otherwise. Don't believe what you hear. Now is the time to make that extra effort to listen to them go on about what "she said, and then he said but she really said," etc. And of course, they are only going to want to talk when you are running late for an important meeting or have dinner for 12 on the stove, but when they open the door to communication, stop and listen. The door may not open again anytime soon.

And speaking of opening doors, the tween years is often when children start shutting doors and want more privacy, claiming they don't need supervision. Giving your children less supervision at this age is a big mistake. The type of supervision they need is different, but this is not the time to let down your guard. Actually, it is quite the opposite. This is the time you need to be more vigilant about knowing where your child is, what he/she is doing, and with whom, at all times. And to add to the challenge, you must do this without your children feeling that you are interfering, spying, not trusting them or withholding responsibility. This is really hard but essential so that you and your child thrive through these tough years.

One of my favorite quotes I have heard from many extremely great parents is "Children will have many friends who come and go in their lives, but they only have one set of parents." You have heard it before, but here it is again: This is not the time to be your child's friend; you must be her parent, which isn't always easy. Parents often say, "My child doesn't want me to volunteer at school any more" or "Mom, you're embarrassing me." Well, that is part of parenting.

And to make things worse, middle schools are not required to have as much supervision for the children compared to elementary schools. The regulations assume that children of this age group are able to be more independent and need less supervision, just as many parents assume. But guess what, this is a really bad idea and may be the cause of why there are so many issues in middle school.

For example, in middle school, students start changing their clothes for physical education (PE) class. Typically, middle schools will have designated locker rooms for boys and girls, and students use lockers to store their personal items, change into PE uniforms or shorts and T-shirts and then meet the PE teacher on the field or in the gym. This is the No. 1 most vulnerable place for problems in a middle school. There is little to no supervision while students are changing, putting away their personal items, etc. If you are looking for a way to improve your child's middle school, volunteer to supervise one of the PE locker rooms. As for all volunteers in a school, you will need to go through a finger-printing and background check to work with students on the campus, but it is worth the time and effort. They really need the help.

Middle school—a whole new ball game

Most parents tell me that parenting their children through elementary school wasn't always easy but they made it through. Then their children enter middle school and the parents realize how different middle school is and how overwhelmed they feel. There is a huge difference between elementary school and middle school, so expect a big transition for you and your child. Middle schools are a "system" like any other and you need to learn how to work within this new "system" to get the best education for your child. This book will give you lots of tips and tricks to master this "system" and get the most out of it to benefit your family.

Elementary schools are the beginning of formal education (of course, parents are the first teachers) for children and therefore make a point to help children and families adjust. They often offer resources such as parenting classes, parent resource centers, easy communication vehicles to talk to teachers, lots of communications sent home, encourage community building with other families and just generally are very supportive to parents. In addition, parents tend to be involved and often volunteer for the school's activities when their children attend elementary school and therefore tend to be more closely connected to the kids and families their children are going to school with.

Middle schools are a whole new ball game. First off, middle schools are often much larger than elementary schools. A typical elementary school will tend to have between 200 and 600 students. In contrast, a typical middle school may have as many as 1,000 students with kids coming from all parts of the city. This can be really scary for students as well as their parents. You have just gone from being a big fish in a small pond, to being a guppy in a sea of unknown sea creatures.

In middle school, you no longer drop your child off at the classroom, so rarely have the opportunity to "run into" the teacher for a quick discussion. And the principal and vice principal are extremely busy, so they aren't available for a drop-in chat. If there is an issue, they would much rather you make an appointment, and even those may be difficult to get.

In middle school children have five to six teachers a day vs. one as they did in elementary school. So chatting with the teacher as your drop off your child doesn't work anymore. Parents often find it a challenge to communicate with their children's teachers in middle school. Some teachers like to communicate through voice mail; others will respond only if you send them an e-mail, and some would prefer that you come in to meet with them in person. In my experience, I have found that most middle-school teachers are extremely dedicated to helping their students, but given that they teach six classes a day, often in multiple subjects, they have to put some limits on their communications with parents. Yet this limit setting sure doesn't feel very good as a parent when you have a concern about your child.

I have often heard middle-school administrators and staff explain to parents that their child isn't the only child in the school. As a parent, that is the last thing you want to hear, even though it is true. But as a parent it is your job to be the advocate for your child in a hectic middle school. If you don't, who else will? The section of this book on "Schools" will give you a number of suggestions for working through these issues.

Who is this hormonal alien that was once my loving child?

Emotionally, middle school is a confusing time for students as well as their parents. Suddenly, they are no longer the leaders of the school as they were in their elementary environment. They are at the bottom of the totem pole again. And sixth grade isn't as kind as kindergarten. The pressures of middle school are completely different. Academic pressure, as well as social pressure, is difficult for many students. Often, I find myself sharing my own experiences in middle school with students who are struggling. We talk about how difficult it is to find your place in middle school when you feel so awkward inside. On the flip side, I am able to share with them how I made it through middle school and that life as an adolescent only got better from there; that my years in high school were much easier and more satisfying. The message of hope is important. There will be more on this topic in the "Stages of Development" section of this book. This will help parents understand what their kids are going through at this age so that you can help them find their ray of hope to get through it.

This book can be used as a reference tool as certain situations come up while your child navigates his or her way through adolescence. You can read the sections of the book that currently apply to you and your family as a way of quickly implementing solutions for a specific issue. It makes great "middle of the night" reading when you are up worrying about something going on with your child. You will find support, humor and specific strategies to help ease your mind and try a different approach.

Another way to use this book is to read it straight through as a way of preparing yourself for what may be coming. Each situation won't apply to every child. But adolescence is a process, so having the tools offered in this book as part of your parenting tool kit will help you see situations while they are still developing. Then you'll have some ideas to try out when the time is right.

Children develop at varying rates, so as parents, we need to do whatever we can to be ready for what may come. The information in this book could apply to your child as early as age 7. If your child is a little bit of a late bloomer, the strategies in this book may be most useful when your child is a teenager, age 15-18. Yet, no matter what your child's development pattern, the transition to middle school is a challenge. The more help we have as parents, the better.

The exciting news is that middle school is a place where your child will do a lot of growing and learning. Over these three years, you will see remarkable changes—some you will like and others you may not. The important thing to remember about this time in your child's life is that it is a journey, not a destination. The changes that occur during middle school are part of the journey toward becoming an adult. This is only the beginning of the process, and there are many years ahead to fine-tune the final product: your child as an adult. This book will offer you many suggestions to help you and your child on this journey. To begin, here are a few tips to keep in mind as you are reading and living these situations. Nothing your child does is meant to you hurt you personally. Remember, they are just children. Don't give up. And on the really difficult days, pull out the baby book and remind yourself how simply adorable your child once was.

Chapter 2

Stages of development— early teen years (ages 10-13)

As parents you know that all children develop differently during every stage of growth. This concept holds true for the stages of development during the "tween" years. Yet there are definitely some typical milestones and phases of development that most children go through during these years, even if the timing and severity of the behavior or growth show up differently for each child.

The purpose of this section is to give an overview of these developmental stages so that you will recognize them when they show up in your home. If you are able to recognize these signs of development early and have some strategies for dealing with them, these transitions will go more smoothly for both you and your child.

Parenthood is unpredictable, but I want to arm you with as much knowledge about this age group as possible so you can be somewhat prepared for what may be coming next. I find that staying half a step ahead of my child makes all the difference in my ability to react effectively, so I hope this section of the book will give you that edge as well. If your child is already in the middle of these developmental stages, keep reading, as many more specific strategies to handle these situations are included in the later chapters of the book.

Entering adolescence isn't easy for anyone, children or parents. It is a time of change and growth. It is a time for children to stretch their wings and see whether they can fly. But that first plunge out of the nest is scary and steep. Additionally, children often feel that they have to cover up the odd or awkward feelings they are experiencing. So do your best to keep the lines of communication open with your child and be ready to talk when he or she is, as the opportunity comes infrequently, most likely at an inconvenient time.

I remember when my son was a toddler and my pediatrician told me that when he was having a tantrum, to try to think about the basic needs and identify which one he wasn't getting at that moment: Was he tired? Or hungry? Did he need a hug? Well, it is very similar during the beginning of adolescence. Your child may be acting out and not able to tell you what is really going on. Take a minute to assess the situation and determine whether one of the basic needs is not being met. As their bodies change during adolescence, children's basic needs will change. They will eat differently, have different sleeping patterns and need comfort in a different way. If you can take a step back from reacting to your child's behavior and give some thought to which basic need may be lacking at that moment, it may help disarm the situation quickly. A snack or a good hug can go a long way when your adolescent is having trouble coping.

What is adolescence?

According to the Merriam-Webster dictionary, the official definition of adolescence is the state or process of growing up, a stage of development prior to maturity. Sounds simple enough, right? Well, we all know adolescence is anything but simple.

Adolescence is the time in life when you work to figure out who you are as an individual, apart from and as part of your family. Adolescence is also the time when hormones increase slowly and steadily until a child matures into an adult Middle school is when this process begins, and there are sure to be ups and downs along the way. I challenge you to think back to when you were in middle school and what your struggles were. Parents often say they don't want their kids to experience the same tough times that they did. I understand wanting to protect your children, but at the same time, it is necessary to go through adolescence to become an adult. Personally, my goal as a parent is to help my children develop into independent adults who make worthwhile contributions to society. That goal may seem lofty when you have an awkward teen who doesn't want to do anything but sit in his room and listen to loud music. But keep your eye on the prize, and the most difficult teenagers can and will turn out to be amazing adults. I encourage you to support and love your children through this period even if they seem unlovable a lot of the time.

Adolescence is a time when children need you most but are least likely to admit it. In fact, this phase in development is very similar to the "Terrible Twos." Remember when your child turned 2 and wanted to do everything himself or herself? Were your child's first words "Me do" and "No," like mine? Adolescence is similar in many ways. Children want their independence but still really need their parents. They want to do things on their own but don't always have the ability. They want to tell you something but can't find the words. They want to fit in with their friends yet still have your approval. Not an easy time for anyone involved.

Below are some of the typical characteristics shown at the various development stages that take place during the middle-school years. Later on in this chapter, you will find more specifics by grade and how these behaviors apply to a child's time in middle school.

Please keep in mind that these descriptions of character included here are for average children in this age group. If your child has a developmental or physiological problem, these descriptions may not fit. There are a lot of resources and help for these children. I recommend you find local resources specific to their needs.

Physical developments

Children grow in various ways and at varying rates of speed. This variety can cause a lot of angst for middle-school students, as their main goal is to fit in, not to be different in any way. A child who sprouts up early may feel quite awkward being the tallest in the class for example. A boy who is the shortest may feel equally weird and may even be the subject of teasing or bullying.

Another issue is that children often grow unevenly. For instance, their hands, feet and limbs tend to grow first while the rest of the body takes some time to catch up. The result is they often look out of proportion and awkward. This growth also tends to affect a child's balance and agility, so middle-school students are often clumsy. This can be devastating to a child who is doing everything he or she can think of to be cool. Most children's growth tends to average out and get to a size that is within a normal range eventually, but the road to get there may seem long for them and even longer for you.

Feel Like a '10'

A friend once shared a story about the awkward feelings that come with development during adolescence. The story was about an 11-year-old girl who felt different from her peers. She was short, wore glasses, had braces and exhibited no signs of developing a womanly figure as her friends were. She often complained to her mother that she felt ugly all the time and wanted to know why her skin was breaking out. Her mom explained that all children develop differently, that what she was experiencing was normal and that she would get through it. As you can imagine, that didn't make much of an impact for this unhappy 11-year-old. Her mom then told her that no matter how she felt about herself right then, she really was a "10" in every way. Her mom explained that she knew this because her daughter had received a perfect 10 score on her tests when she was born. Her mom reassured her that with this perfect 10 beginning she was bound to blossom into a perfect and beautiful young lady, a true 10. My friend was that awkward-feeling 11-year-old who never forgot what her mom told her about being a perfect "10." This encouragement gave her hope that she carried into being a confident young woman who is still a perfect 10 in her mom's eyes. Developing into an adolescent isn't easy, but anything we can do to give our children hope and reassurance goes a long way.

Psychological development

Middle-school students are often erratic and inconsistent in their behavior due to the psychological changes taking place in their development. The word "drama" comes to mind often when talking about this age group. Life situations tend to become very dire and extreme with middle-school students. It's all part of the growing process. Nevertheless, this erratic behavior can be very disconcerting for parents. Middle-school students don't always share their inspirations and thoughts with parents, so their actions and behaviors often come as a surprise. What can you do? Stay flexible and use the mantra adopted by many middle- school educators: "Never Say Never." Just when you think you understand your son or daughter, this person enters adolescence and does something that seems completely out of character. Keep in mind, this behavior isn't always bad, just different, unexpected, and can really throw you for a loop.

Trying on new likes, dislikes, interests, even personalities, is all part of the psychological development process they must go through to figure out who they will become as adults. Be patient and kind; these behaviors will become more predictable in a few years. Your reaction can really fuel the interest in creating drama, so staying calm, cool and collected during this time will help defuse some of the behaviors faster than anything else.

This is a time when children are searching for a new, more adult-like identity as well as acceptance from peers. Keep in mind that your child has been studying your adult identity for years unconsciously and eventually will adopt much of what he or she has seen, even without realizing it. And many children may try out a few new ideas that they have seen or learned about out in the world along the way.

Experimenting goes along with the territory of growing up, so you can expect that your child will definitely experiment. The question will be what they will experiment with and when. This is such a prominent part of adolescence that there is an entire chapter dedicated to experimenting later in the book. But in the meantime, you should know that experimenting is simply part of the process. Experimenting is one of those areas in which parents have to dig deep and take confidence in knowing that the many years of hard work you have put into laying a strong foundation of good morals and values will stand the test of time.

During this time you may see your child striving to be more mature yet, at the same time, becoming extremely sensitive. You'll notice that children of this age are easily offended and often get their feelings hurt by those around them—their family, friends, teachers and others. This hyper-sensitivity can be frustrating for parents. One minute your child is begging for more responsibility and asking not to be treated like a child, and in the next breath, he or she is devastated at the way you looked at him/her from across the breakfast table. Do yourself a favor and don't try to make sense of this behavior; just chalk it up to this stage in life. There will be more specific ideas and suggestions on this topic in the "Parenting and home life" chapter of this book.

Social development

This may be the most frustrating area of development for parents of a middle-school student. All of a sudden your children seem to care more about what their friends think than you. During this social development, conflicts are bound to arise due to your children's loyalties to their peers and how their behavior and decision making may be in conflict with your family rules and values. Children at this age will start looking to their peers as role models instead of you. And are these the role models you really want for your child? Probably not. This shift can be scary, but again if you have given your child a strong foundation, he or she will make it through this stage and fall back on those good values and judgment eventually.

At times children become rebellious toward their parents during middle school yet are still strongly dependent on their approval. This may seem confusing to parents, but the reality is that adolescence is confusing for you and your child. Your child will start having new impulses and thoughts that are different from anything previously experienced. I find the best way to make sense of these social developments is to remember that there is a strong internal conflict going on inside your child that is causing this external behavior that seems so odd and often uncharacteristic.

Intellectual development

Middle-school students are intensely curious, but they want to learn things they consider useful or relevant to the real world. This presents a great challenge for educators, teachers, administrators and people who create curriculum standards for our education system. There are capable, caring teachers out there who will take the curriculum standards for this age group and make these concepts come alive to today's adolescents. Then there are other teachers who don't. They teach the curriculum in the same fashion it has been taught for years, and therefore middle-school students may have trouble finding the relevance of the concepts to their lives. This will also be a challenge at home, as children will wonder how doing their chores on a weekly basis is going to help them achieve their goal of becoming a professional football player, for example.

This search for relevance can show up in a change of attitude in which children feel as if they know more than the influential adults in their lives. The know-it-all attitude can be annoying and seem disrespectful in the moment. I am in no way suggesting that a child should ever be given permission to be disrespectful to parents and/or teachers, but I believe there is a way to work through this attitude in which children feel validated and still understand that they are part of an interconnected system, not the nucleus.

Moral and ethical development

Children this age have a strong sense of fairness. A popular phrase used in middle school is, "But that's not fair!" As we all know, life *isn't* always fair, but when you are 12 or 13 years old and trying to make sense of the adult world you are entering, one can see how this phrase has gained popularity. Dealing with life situations, even if they aren't fair, comes down to taking responsibility for yourself and your actions. This is a mature concept and difficult to grasp when you are an adolescent beginning to face the realities of the world. We all know adults who still struggle with this concept, so imagine how difficult it is for a child.

Another common behavior of children this age is to attempt to test their relationships, particularly with their parents. To test your love and dedication, they will ask hard-to-answer questions like, "What is the meaning of life?" "Is there life after death?" or "Do you believe in God?" Children ask these questions not necessarily to receive an answer but more to test your reactions. Too often parents find these types of questions annoying and will make light of them or provide a meaningless answer like, "Go ask your father." In all honesty, I don't think most children expect an answer to questions like these, but if they get a trivial adult response, their feelings are deeply hurt and the message sent is that their questions are unimportant to you. Of course this couldn't be further from the truth, but it's all part of the process for children to evaluate your love for them during a time they may feel unlovable.

Children talk to their parents a lot less during adolescence, so if your child attempts to talk to you, even if it is only to ask you annoying philosophical questions, don't dismiss the opportunity. Begin a discussion on the meaning of life or whatever else he or she is curious about. Often these questions lead into a very insightful discussion about children's lives. Remember that your son or daughter is confronting hard moral and ethical questions and doesn't yet have the maturity or life experience to know how to deal with these.

Sixth grade

The first week of school you often hear teachers and school staff commenting on the incoming sixth- grade students: "They are so cute"; "They look so young"; "They are so small." All of these things are true. You can spot them a mile away as sixth-graders do tend to be much smaller and look very immature compared with the seventh- and eighth- graders, and often carry backpacks that are bigger than they are. Another way to spot a new sixth-grade student is to watch for kids pulling those cute backpacks on wheels that a seventh- or eighth-grader wouldn't be caught dead with.

The reality is that sixth-graders look too young to be attending a middle school. And maybe they are, but that's another discussion entirely. Most middle-school administrators realize how different sixth-grade students are from seventh- and eighth-grade students, so they make provisions to accommodate their needs.

Many schools have a certain part of their campus dedicated to the classes for sixth-grade students. They often have separate lunch and break schedules. Theoretically, sixth-graders could go to school and rarely interact with their older schoolmates, but most schools have a far from perfect system. Often sixth-graders will have PE classes either mingled with seventh- and eighth-graders or they will have class at the same time, which means they will be dressing in the locker rooms together even if their classes are taught separately. Before school and after school are also times when students of all grades are together on campus with little to no supervision. In the past, schools would offer a safe, constructive place for students to be before and after school such as the library or cafeteria. But many schools have given this up due to budget cuts, so the kids are on their own on campus while they wait for school to start or wait to be picked up by a parent.

I firmly believe there is safety in numbers, so I highly recommend parents of incoming sixth-grade students find a carpool arrangement with neighbors or friends so that your child has a friend to arrive and leave school with. One of the most difficult and possibly vulnerable moments for a sixth-grader (or student of any age) is when being dropped off at school, looking around a large campus and not finding a friendly or familiar face. Carpooling prevents this issue and can often take some load off parents' already hectic schedules.

As for schoolwork, sixth grade tends to start out fairly as sort of a "honeymoon" period for students. Teachers know there are a lot of adjustments when starting middle school, so they usually make a great of effort to help students get used to the new systems and procedures. They don't give a lot of homework or projects. They design assignments with the purpose of teaching students how to navigate middle school and keep it light. The difficulty of the assignments and the amount of homework gradually intensify as school progresses with the hope that the students will be able to ramp up in the same way. As an educator, I feel that this approach is really a mistake. Cognitively, students in sixth grade are primed to learn and often have a better attitude about education than their seventh- and eighth-grade friends. If your school is taking this light approach to education in the sixth grade, consider what educational opportunities you can offer your child outside of school to supplement. Don't hesitate to ask your child's teachers to suggest extra work that may help them keep your student challenged. Your child will be much better prepared academically for future years in school as well as solidifying a love of learning.

Sixth-grade students do a lot of growing emotionally and physically. Girls are typically small and haven't yet developed physically yet. They often still enjoy playing with babyish toys like dolls and horses. Boys in sixth grade are even smaller than girls. They tend to be quite short at this stage and sprout up later. Boys also still enjoy playing with their toys from younger years, such as cars, trains and Legos, but both girls and boys quickly realize that playing with these types of toys may not be cool now that they are in middle school. So they tend to start shying away from these types of toys openly and reserve these play activities for times by themselves or only with a longtime trusted friend. Sad but true.

Sixth-grade girls are desperate for approval from everyone: parents, teachers and friends. This need for approval becomes complex because to get this approval they aren't sure what activities are OK and what behaviors are not. Their impulses don't always align with what they know they are supposed to do, so things get tricky.

Fitting in is also a big theme for sixth-grade girls. In middle school it is hard to tell who is a trendsetter and who is a follower when everyone is seeking approval from the others. Here is where the popularity contest begins.

Boys tend to become less outwardly focused in sixth grade and begin turning inward and often share little with anyone—parents, teachers or friends. Even if they feel overwhelmed, they won't ask for help. Similarly, girls can be very sensitive and timid in sixth grade, especially around adults they don't know well, such as teachers. It takes a very observant teacher to pick up on these issues and offer the help to students even if they don't ask. But again, as class sizes get bigger and expectations of teachers are greater than ever, students feeling overwhelmed may get overlooked.

The love life of a sixth-grader is typically minimal, but brace yourself, as that won't last long. Some girls begin to have interest in boys during sixth grade, but more often than not, they continue friendships with boys at this age and don't have romantic feelings just yet. Even if they do, sixth-grade boys are more inwardly focused so they either don't notice this attention from a girl or just simply don't care. Girls at this age can be very silly and secretive, and boys just don't have any interest in this behavior. There are definitely cases in which girls develop crushes on certain boys, but these crushes rarely turn into anything more than having something fun to talk about with their friends and silly attempts to get the boys' attention. These activities tend to annoy more than flatter boys at this age.

In sixth grade, both girls and boys tend to continue their interest in extracurricular activities such as sports, playing a musical instrument or performing in theatre. These are wonderful outlets for children, and I strongly recommend parents' encouraging their participation. Later in middle school, many students decide these activities aren't the cool thing to do anymore. But if children have no extracurricular activities, they end up having too much time alone and way too much time to design their own, possibly less constructive extracurricular activities. So keep them involved as long as possible.

When your child enters middle school, it is really important to have a strong presence in their daily activities. Supervision is super important at this stage of development for two key reasons. One is that when a child feels insecure, having a parent's participation in his or her activities makes that child feel safe even if the child tells you something different. Secondly, children in sixth grade haven't yet realized that it isn't very cool to have parents hanging around, so they accept your presence without making much of it. This often changes in seventh and eighth grades, so it is a good precedent to set early on.

The trend seems to be that parents start to back off a bit on their participation and direct supervision when their children enter middle school. They often give their children more responsibility and let them do more things independently. I agree that letting children feel that they have more responsibility and independence is a wonderful concept, but balancing those feelings with safety and supervision is very important.

Do what you can to stay involved in your child's activities whether at school, extracurricular, with friends or in other situations. Be the parent who drives the group here and there, and be the one who has the kids over to your house. If you aren't able to personally supervise all of your child's activities, team up with other parents whom you trust to have similar values and judgment. Ask a family member to drive the kids to afterschool activities, or arrange carpools with other parents. If you don't know other families at your school, ask the school administrators or your child's teachers to introduce you to some. Working together with other families will send a strong message to your child that he or she is part of a community that cares about kids. By the time your child gets to seventh grade, he or she may not want you to volunteer at school or coach a sports team, but if you have been doing these things all along, then your child may not think about it as much while getting older.

Seventh grade

During the beginning of the school year, it is so much fun to see how the sixth-graders have transformed into incoming seventh-graders. They grow and change so much during the summer between sixth and seventh grades that the students are almost not recognizable. Seventh-grade boys are often still shorter than the girls, but they are all looking much more grown-up. The girls often begin maturing in the summer between sixth and seventh grades, so they enter the new school year with the beginning signs of becoming young women. Seventh- graders definitely have more confidence and are more self-assured than when they were in sixth grade, but almost all the children look a little awkward in their new skin.

In seventh grade the fashion show begins, especially among the girls. After all, the girls have one another to impress, and now they are also interested in catching the attention of the boys. I highly recommend holding off on the back-to-school shopping trip until school starts. I guarantee they will want some new duds once they see what everyone else is wearing, so don't spend the clothing budget before they go to school and decide what is really in fashion that year. Seventh grade is a time when both boys and girls become more aware of their appearance and may begin spending a lot more time and energy figuring out how they want to look and what they can do to fit in. Given that all the kids are striving to have the fashionable look, it is unclear who the leaders are and who the followers are. This interest in being accepted by others makes it increasingly hard to figure out whether one is "in" or not. This confusion fuels most of the energy spent by middle-school students. It is a constant dance to figure out what is cool and who is setting the trends.

It all comes down to popularity. All kids want to be popular. Being popular means they are accepted widely by their peers, which to a seventh-grader is heaven, or so it seems. Most kids can tell you who is popular and who isn't, but it is never very clear as to what is the formula for becoming popular. This is the ongoing struggle of seventh grade. Ironic isn't it? This idea really defies the definition of popularity but that is middle school for you.

Friendships become a full time job in seventh grade. Boys tend to continue spending time with their long time group of friends, but that group may begin to change. One boy in the group may be accepted into a popular crowd when the others haven't been. This can be very distressing for both the boy who has been deemed popular as well as his friends who have not. He definitely wants to hang out with the popular group—who wouldn't? But he feels disloyal to his old group whom he has grown up with. Seventh-grade boys tend to roll with peer issues fairly well, so these situations will often work themselves out. Girls, on the other hand, are a different story. Friendships become their obsession, and they become extremely sensitive if a friend appears to be disloyal. And girls will hold a grudge for years, whereas boys move on from an issue quite quickly. I was once helping a group of seventh-grade girls get through some issues they were having and asked one of them to tell me when this issue began. The first words out of her mouth were "in second grade, she said...." Second grade? The disagreement they were having was carried over from second grade. Talk about holding a grudge. Read the chapter of this book on "Peers" to learn much more about this community that may seem to take over your child's life during the years of middle school.

The term "boy crazy" tends to come to mind when talking about seventh-grade girls, yet most boys their age don't feel the same. The good news for parents is that these crushes tend to be short-lived and don't typically turn into anything substantial. Girls develop crushes easily and often. Every seventh-grade girl will probably have a crush on someone, whether it is a classmate, someone's older brother, a teacher or a neighbor. The fact is, girls at this age fall hard. It is common for girls to even have a type of crush on other girls. For instance, your daughter may admire, even idolize, another girl within her group of friends. Again, these crushes are typically harmless, but don't underestimate the amount of time and energy girls put into them. Crushes like these can be all-consuming to a seventh-grade girl. It is a wonder that students retain any knowledge they learn in seventh grade, as their brains are so consumed with other things.

Boys often continue their extracurricular activities through seventh grade such as sports, Boy Scouts or music. Unfortunately, girls tend to drop these interests during this stage of development. They become so consumed with keeping up with their friends and talking on the phone that they often lose interest in more structured activities. Dropping these types of activities is a slippery slope many times, resulting in kids with too much time on their hands and not enough supervision. So, do whatever you can to encourage your child to continue participating in structured activities as long as possible. A busy preteen is a good preteen. Children become lethargic at this stage of development. There are so many changes going on in their bodies that they have less energy for physical activity and feel that they need more time to themselves to sort out these changes. Yet the more interest middle school students have outside of the phone and Instant Messenger or Facebook, the better. Having too much time alone can cause preteens to feel depressed and lonely. Conversely, spending too much time with peers can also have a negative effect, as kids this age need a balanced perspective, not just influence from their friends. Peer relationships are rocky during this time, so you don't want your child's only activity outside of school to be keeping up with the latest gossip. Having other social and activity outlets will help give them balance and perspective. Plus, physical activity can help with fitness, health and self-esteem.

In most middle schools, seventh-graders are in the position of a middle child at school. They aren't the excited babies of sixth grade or the extremely cool and know-it-all eighth-graders. Seventh-graders often find it difficult to shine. I think it is helpful when seventh-grade students develop friendships with students in their own grade rather than trying to fit in with either sixth- or eighth-graders. Most schools are set up in such a way that they have little interaction with students of other grades, but I find this is a good thing for parents to be aware of. If your child is gravitating toward kids in other grades, you may want to look closer to see what issues he or she may be having with kids of the same age.

Communication with a seventh-grader can be challenging. Some boys will find it easier to communicate with adults and teachers at this age. They often find a voice and are willing to try it out. Girls, on the other hand, tend to go more inward with their communication during seventh grade. They often talk less with parents and teachers but a lot more with their peers. Having peers as a dominant influence on your child is a scary prospect, so make sure you know whom they are becoming friends with, what they are doing and whom they are doing it with at all times. Girls of this age still want their parents' approval, but at times it may go on the back burner in the pursuit of popularity.

The changes that go on when your child reaches seventh grade may be a bit shocking at first. It is often the beginning of what adolescence will evolve into over the next few years. I suggest parents roll with the changes a little bit. Never compromise on what you know is right for your children, and never stop supervising their activities, but realize that there are lots of changes going on and your child probably feels as uncomfortable about them as you do. Parents get the brunt of children's awkward feelings, as home is usually a safe place to let it all out, whereas school isn't. Give your child the space and compassion needed right now. Most importantly, don't take your child's behavior personally. It is not a direct reflection on you or your parenting skills. Your reaction to this behavior is what is most important and how you and your child will continue a strong connection even through these stages of great change. And to help keep your sanity, pick the battles that are most important during this stage of development. Purple hair will eventually grow out, and the natural consequences that your child will experience while having purple hair (such as being made fun of at school) will go much further than your yelling and screaming about it.

Eighth grade

If you take a picture of a child starting in the sixth grade and then compare it with a picture of that same child at the beginning of eighth grade, you may not recognize it as the same child. Children grow and mature rapidly over the three years in middle school and by the time they reach eighth grade, many children look awfully mature. Eighth-grade students can often be mistaken for high school students. The boys have finally caught up to the girls in height, and both boys and girls have developed more adult-like features—facial hair for boys, breasts for girls. And of course, the dreaded first signs of acne often show up in children starting eighth grade.

Along with entering eighth grade comes a new attitude. This is the attitude that makes parents crazy. The eighth-grade attitude is the know-it-all, "I don't need help from anyone" attitude. This is the attitude that comes with that head shake, rolling eyes and hip movement that make parents think, "Where did they learn this?" when they first see it. Eighth-graders often become bossy and disagreeable, especially at home. At school the theme is "be cool," and this attitude can look disrespectful to teachers and school staff. But as an eighth-grader you must be cool at all times and in all situations. You must wear cool clothes, do cool things, eat cool foods and hang out with cool people. The struggle is that all the kids are trying to be cool, but no one is exactly sure what is considered cool in every situation. Most kids spend a lot of time worrying about the choices they are making, second-guessing what others will think is cool and then feeling awkward if they haven't made the coolest decision. Now, of course, an eighth-grade student would never admit to having this internal struggle, as they know everything. So they often try to handle these feelings by themselves, which then brings up other issues, typically displayed at home.

Eighth-graders are the leaders of the school who are looked up to as well as feared by the younger sixth- and seventh-grade students. This is a powerful position that some students thrive in and others try to use to their advantage. Being in eighth grade gives some students the idea that they can bully others or pick on students younger and in a less powerful position. Yet some students see eighth grade as an opportunity to be leaders and offer positive role models for the younger students.

Students in eighth grade feel more mature than their years. They are striving to be adults in many ways and therefore, tend to expect the freedom and independence of adults. This new attitude often causes conflict between parents and tweens. Eighth-graders don't think they need supervision and expect their parents to allow them quite a bit of freedom. Yet this is definitely not the time to relax your standards on supervising your children. It is still extremely important that you know where your child is at all times, whom they are with and what they are doing. They aren't going to like this, but for their safety it is a must.

But eighth grade is a good time for kids to take on more responsibility, especially with the household chores and reaching out to help others. Many schools have programs for eighth-grade students to help younger students. They can tutor students in subjects they excel in, help out in elementary school classrooms, introduce new students to the school, raise funds for school activities. Helping others is a perfect way to keep the eighth-grade attitude under control as well as channel their time and energy in positive ways. Helping out at home is a must, and I encourage you to give your children increasing responsibility there as long as it is age appropriate. Don't expect that by assigning an eighth-grader, chores that they will remember to do them in a timely manner and that they will do them happily. But it is good for them to be reminded that they are part of a family unit and therefore must share in the work that comes with that. Check the family and home life chapter of the book for much more on this topic.

Drama is a continuous theme in middle school, but the amount of drama seems to escalate exponentially in the eighth grade. All situations tend to be a disaster or an event of huge proportion. The highs and lows come quickly and often. The best approach for parents is to stay on an even keel as much as possible. It is important to listen and show support for the dramatic feelings your child may be having, but I also would recommend trying not getting too caught up in the drama, as the situation will change the minute you do so.

Children's social lives also seem to escalate in the eighth grade. Boys are now equally interested in girls, so there seems to be an emphasis on activities that they can do together: activities such as parties, trips to the mall, going to the movies. In fact, eighth-graders spend so much time and energy strategizing these plans that they often want to drop other extracurricular activities that they have enjoyed. They tend to drop sports, music or other interests so they can devote all of their free time to worrying about who is going to what party and what they are going to wear. This can be a slippery slope in spending so much of your energy worrying about what other people think and whether you are making the right choices to get approval from someone else. This type of activity does nothing toward maintaining a healthy self-esteem. Please do whatever you can to help your child find a balance between participating in the social life of eighth grade and doing what pleases him or her personally. Also, keep in mind that a busy adolescent is a good adolescent. In other words, keeping children interested in positive structured activities will ensure that their time and energy are being used well. They will also be more efficient in doing homework and fulfilling responsibilities at home. When kids of this age have too much time on their hands, they don't tend to spend it very wisely.

And just when eighth-graders are feeling really confident and at the top of their game, it is time to graduate and move on to high school. Leaving middle school can bring on as much anxiety and apprehension as entering. For students who have struggled to find their place during the middle-school years, there may be a sense of hope that moving to high school will open up new opportunities. High schools often offer more diversity and therefore more opportunities to be accepted. Yet there are often the anxious feelings that come with the unknown.

For the students who are now enjoying their positions of power as leaders in their middle school, the idea of giving up that status and starting all over again in high school can be daunting.

Graduation

Some of my favorite times in middle school were chaperoning for the eighth-grade graduation dance. The kids all looked so adorable, cleaned up and showing off their best duds. The dance seemed to be going along well. The decorations were festive, the music was fun, and most of the kids were dancing. Yet as the event came to a close, the most interesting thing happened. The D.J. announced the last song of the evening and as the kids were dancing, all of the girls started crying. I mean really crying. At first it started out with just a few, but the feeling seemed to be contagious and before I knew it, they were all crying. The boys were trying to be sweet in consoling these sobbing girls, and then some of them starting crying too. It was a complete water works! An entire middle-school gym of smeared mascara and flying Kleenex. I started to ask some of the kids why everyone was crying. They gave me a list of detailed reasons: This girl is going to a different high school than her best friend; another girl broke up with her boyfriend because she was leaving for camp the next day; someone else didn't get a chance to dance with the boy she has a crush on. The reasons were all clearly valid and very upsetting to these kids, but what I came to realize is that this is just what you do at the end of middle school: cry.

Chapter 3

Motivation

As hormone levels increase, preteens experience lots of changes, both physically and mentally. These changes affect many areas of their lives, including their energy levels and motivation. A number of factors go into a lack of motivation. One is a shift in energy level as the day goes on. Because preteens often have trouble sleeping, they tend to be tired at odd times of the day, such as first thing in the morning or right after lunch. Yet they are wide awake late at night when they really should be going to sleep, causing disruption in their regular sleep cycle. This poor sleeping pattern causes many middle-school students to struggle to stay engaged during their classes. It can also cause problems with their participation in extracurricular activities such as sports. Sports teams often hold practices and games after school, in the evenings and early in the morning on the weekends Children who aren't getting a good night's rest may not have much energy or motivation to play sports during their down times of the day. And the vicious cycle continues.

Sleep isn't the only factor at play here. Preteens experience a type of lethargy, which can look like laziness. Not only are their bodies changing rapidly, but also their minds are full of new ideas that can be confusing and contradictory to anything they have ever thought before. This brain overload can cause kids to want to retreat to a safe place to sort these thoughts out. None of this is conscious behavior, but watch closely as you will start seeing the signs.

And then add hormones into the mix and you've got quite a mess on your hands.

To help illustrate what this behavior change looks like, I will tell you about a seventh-grade girl I used to work with named Monica. Up until seventh grade, she was very active, lively and genuinely involved in everything she did be it schoolwork, playing with friends or hanging out with her family. During the summer after sixth grade, she grew a ton. Her mom said she had grown over 2½ inches in the summer months alone. Her body looked a bit lanky now as she had gotten really tall and thin and her arms and legs looked out of proportion to the rest of her.

Monica's mom called me asking for guidance as her daughter was acting strange in her opinion. At first, Monica's mom thought she might have the flu, so she took her to see the doctor, but he confirmed that everything was normal. When Monica seemed to show flulike symptoms over and over, her mom started thinking that maybe this was something else, like adolescence. And sure enough, symptoms that look like the flu—fatigue, moodiness, lethargy, lack of motivation, need to sleep in, hunger but uncertainty about what to eat—are all typical for an adolescent who is perfectly healthy.

This may be a time when your child would prefer to spend more time in his or her room alone. Preteens sometimes want to create a cave-like environment in their rooms and may request adding their own phones or televisions in there. Your child may complain about spending time with the family eating meals or going along for family outings.

It may feel as if this child suddenly wants to shut you and the other family members out of his or her life. Preteens often give only one-word answers to questions about their day. It's common for them to want to drop out of groups or organizations in which they have enjoyed participating in the past.

Having a child with a lack of motivation can be one of the greatest challenges for parents. When children begin their retreat and pulling away from their families and activities, parents often get frustrated and sad, which often leads to anger and throwing in the towel. Talking to your child probably won't work, but it is worth a try. When children go through this stage of life, they often don't want to share things with their parents. They would rather turn to their peers who are having the same issues.

Parents often misunderstand this new behavior and take it personally. So often they try giving children what they ask for, such as their own phone and/or television in their room, hoping to help bridge the gap they feel growing between themselves and their child. This is a wonderful intention, but it doesn't work. In fact, giving in to your preteen's unreasonable requests may cause more damage to your long-term relationship with your child instead of bringing you closer in the short term.

Children going through adolescence are not mad at their parents, but they are confused and frustrated with the world. So they take it out on their families because that is a safe environment for them whereas the outside world is not a safe place for them to truly express themselves yet. Although preteens have the urge to spend time alone, they need more supervision than ever. Putting a phone, television or computer in your child's room makes it very difficult for you to supervise those activities. And if your child has a cell phone, the main purpose for that phone should be for you to communicate with him or her. So, when at home, I suggest given the cell phone a parking place so that there isn't constant distraction with calls/texts at home. A drawer in the kitchen or a place near the door is a convenient location to store a cell phone until your child goes out again.

Depression can also play a factor. If your child is showing some of these signs, it may be difficult to figure out whether this behavior is normal adolescence or your child is struggling with depression. Consulting with your pediatrician is a good idea if your child seems suddenly and inexplicably sad or withdrawn.

Staying connected

Asking your child questions is no longer the way to gain insight into how he or she is feeling. Instead, try spending time with your child doing things that he or she is interested in to gain insight into what your child is thinking and feeling during this difficult time of development. Driving in the car is another great place for heart-to-heart conversations, but let your child initiate the discussion. Don't try to force a conversation. There seems to be some comfort in talking about difficult subjects if you don't have to actually be face to face, such as while riding in a car. Most importantly, if you are there and available, your child will open up to you eventually; it just will be on their schedule, not yours. And of course it will usually occur when you are rushing to get someplace or have 10 other important things on your mind. I know it is really difficult, but I strongly recommend stopping whatever else is going on at that moment and giving your child undivided attention. They don't open up often at this age, so when they do, take advantage of the opportunity.

Keeping kids active

Even if your child says he doesn't want to do things with the family or participate in activities, this is one of the most important ways of keeping children connected during adolescence. If they don't have this connection at home or in a positive place, they will look for it in other places that may not be as positive.

Leadership fosters action

Remember how you used "reverse psychology" when your child was a toddler throwing tantrums? You may have let her think that she made the decision as to what to do next when, in reality, she only chose from the acceptable options you gave.

A very similar approach works well to get your preteen motivated into action.

First you must give children some responsibility for something that is important to them. For instance, most preteens want to have some say in what the family is going to do or the activities that are being forced upon them.

A weekly family meeting can go a long way toward figuring out what it is your preteen wants. Then give your son or daughter some responsibility to make sure it happens. Set a specific time each week for a family meeting. Or better yet, allow your preteen to set the time and insist that all members of the family must attend. Each family member should take a turn leading the meeting and creating the weekly agenda. Here is a list of some things you may consider adding to your agenda.

- Compliments
- Calendar
- Family fun
- Upcoming events/planning
- Weekly household assignments
- Check-in

When issues come up during the week, suggest the child add it to the agenda for the next family meeting. Family meetings are a wonderful time to brainstorm solutions to problems as well as time to share information. It is also a really great excuse for all family members to come together at least once a week.

It won't take long for your children to see that participating in the decision-making process for the family will help them get more of what they ultimately want. And, therefore, it won't take long until they are very motivated to participate in the family meetings as a leader (not just a forced participant) as well as become more of a leader in life outside of the family meetings.

Finding passion

There is often a lot of drama surrounding the lives of middle-school students, so I suggest that you do your best to channel the dramatics into something that may really help motivate your child during this time in their life and on into the future. Helping them find and foster their passion for something can be really powerful. Often kids of this age become passionate about something parents don't think is useful so their passions are often pushed aside. For instance, your child may be really interested in Anime shows and characters. This may seem like a teenage fad to you, but it could be a great way to spark interest and creativity in your child. He could begin drawing Anime characters to find the artist within or attend an Anime conference and grow his social skills or discover a more global view of the world, as Anime may be created far from home. These are just some examples of positive things that can come from a trendy interest your son/daughter may have. Do what you can to ignite your child's passions and encourage positive activities to go along with these passions. Supporting your children in this way will go a long way in keeping a close connection between you as well as keeping them motivated in all parts of their lives.

Girl Talk on Politics

At one time, I ran weekly groups for girls at a middle school were I worked. It was a drop in-group where the girls and I would have lunch together and talk. We called it "Girl Talk". The regulars ended up being a good size group of bright young ladies with a lot to say. Topics of discussion were never hard to come by. I was fortunate enough to hold this group one year during a US Presidential election. The election came up in discussion a number of times. The girls were very passionate about the right to vote. They couldn't understand why they weren't allowed to participate. We talked about the many struggles through American history for different groups of people to vote, including women. I had to be the bearer of bad news and explain that our constitution regards them too young to vote. One young lady said to me "why are we too young to vote? We are the ones in school learning about politics and government. By the time you get older and become parents you forget everything you learn in school." She definitely has a point. Another young lady explained to me that if she could vote, she would vote for the candidate that wants to end legalized abortions. That began a fascinating discussion among these young woman about the right to choose vs. what is legal or not. I was amazed at how aware these middle school students were on topics that most adults consider highly sophisticated. It is a lesson to us all to never underestimate young people and their ability to contribute to our society. I have heard many adults discount the abilities of middle school students as it is considered an awkward time in life. My experience has been the exact opposite. If given the chance, young people in this age group are very capable and willing to make their contributions.

Chapter 4

Health

Keeping children healthy when they reach middle-school age is much different from when they were younger. They no longer tell you when there is something wrong or that they genuinely don't feel well. They are more private about their bodies and more independent in taking care of themselves, so an obvious sign of something wrong may not be so obvious to you anymore.

This chapter focuses on the large preventive areas of health: nutrition, hygiene, exercise and sleep. There are obviously other health-related issues that may come up, and if they do, you should never hesitate to talk to your child's physician. This may also be a good time to give your child permission to talk to the physician by herself, if this hasn't already occurred. This may also be a good time to change to a doctor whom your child feels most comfortable with. For example, a preteen girl may prefer to have a female doctor vs. a male. A professional, caring opinion can be wonderful for a child with lots of questions and/or concerns about what may or may not be happening with his or her body. As a parent, it is important for you to stay out of these conversations unless your child asks you to be there. The doctor will let you know if there is an area for concern, but if not, it may be more effective for your child to be able to share concerns with the doctor confidentially.

Nutrition

Adolescents are not exactly known for keeping a healthy diet. In fact most middle-school-age children have pretty bad eating habits. Changes in hormones cause adolescents to actually crave foods that are not healthy. They tend to want fried, high-fat, high-sugar foods. Most of us made it through adolescence fairly healthy despite making unhealthy diet choices, so I wouldn't make your child's diet your highest concern, but I hope this information will give you some insight and ideas. With that said, if healthy eating has been an issue prior to hitting adolescence, I recommend talking with your child's doctor about the best way to get a handle of this situation now. More and more children are having health-related issues due to poor nutrition. If this has been going on for a while, it will only get worse, so try to be as proactive as possible to help your child make positive changes.

Let's start with lunch. Lunchtime at a middle school could best be described as barely organized chaos. There are lines for everything and kids everywhere. Most schools have either a designated area for lunch or a cafeteria. Either way, it is a lot of kids in a small space with a lot of activity and noise.

First off, there are the school lunches. These are the pre-made meals offered by the school district for a low price. The line for the school lunches is short because they look and taste terrible. A monthly menu is published, and it includes foods that kids typically like; for instance, hot dogs, hamburgers, tacos, pizza, burritos, etc. These items are alternated throughout the school calendar. These may be the types of foods that tend to appeal to kids of this age group, but the actual food isn't very tasty. These are definitely not the hamburgers you get at McDonald's or the hot dogs sold at the ballpark. There is an attempt to add a nutritious component to the lunches—a cup of fruit cocktail or a package of dried-up mini-carrots. You can guess where those end up.

The school cafeterias redeem themselves one day a month and serve creamed turkey over mashed potatoes. The kids groan on that day, but the school staff loves it. A reminder of a hot lunch of comfort food from the past, yet still very high in calories and low in nutritional value. You can hear a buzz in the school office on the day creamed turkey and mashed potatoes are served. Get your order in quickly because they sell out often. But on every other day, the line for the school lunches is the shortest and much of it ends up in the garbage.

The next area of the lunchroom is dedicated to the "a la carte" menu. Each school has its own label for this area, but this is where kids can buy the food they really want. Name-brand pizza, french fries, chips, sugary drinks in strange colors and popular candy bars. As you can imagine, these lines are very long. This is what kids want to eat. This is also what is considered "cool" to eat. It isn't considered "cool" to like healthy foods that your mom or dad sends with you to school.

On a positive note, lunch is only one meal of the day. You may not be able to deter your children from wanting or eating the junk food sold at lunchtime, but you can have some influence over the other times they eat. What you offer them for breakfast, dinner and snacks at home becomes much more important. Here are some ideas.

Morning is a hectic time in many households, so breakfast ends up being skipped or turned into a to-go meal. But many of the fast breakfast foods on the market are full of calories and sugar. These may give your child a quick start in the morning, but by second period, he or she may have trouble paying attention in class or even staying awake. Here are some ideas for making the most of breakfast. Think protein and think ahead. A peanut butter and jelly sandwich on wheat bread is an excellent choice for a fast on-the-run nutritious breakfast. A hard-boiled egg and/or string cheese is another good choice. Even pre-made peanut butter crackers are better than a bowl of sugared cereal. A glass of milk, even chocolate milk, will provide a lot of protein and vitamins in the morning. This may also help settle a nervous stomach, which seems to be a fairly common occurrence for middle-school students.

Try sending a snack along with your child to school. Most middle schools offer a morning break. If your child didn't get the best breakfast or even if she did, you can offer another chance at some good food to eat during the break. A granola bar with nuts or some trail mix made with dried fruit, banana chips and almonds are a few ideas. Your child may tell you he doesn't want or need to bring a snack to school. Just stick it into his backpack anyway. By midmorning, he may be glad to have it. I also recommend throwing in a bottle of water as well. Your child may love the strange colored drinks sold at lunch, but in between some water is a really good idea.

Next is the dreaded after-school, sit-in- front- of- the-TV-and-eat issue. The best thing you can do for your children after school is to get them involved in something. Kids are tired after school, and zoning out in front of a TV eating high- calorie snacks may seem very appealing if left to their own devices. Yet if you ask a child who does that on a regular basis, she will admit being bored spending the afternoons in the company of TV shows such as MTV. The after-school hours are when middle-school students are at highest risk for a number of things, including poor nutrition. See Chapter 6 for more on supervision ideas for your kids, but beware that this is often a time when needless eating and laziness occur.

As for dinner, a busy schedule may not allow your family to have dinner together every night, but see what you can do to schedule a family dinner at least one or two nights a week. At times, dinner is the only time the family actually sits down together and connects. This is very important for nutrition as well as preserving a strong relationship with your children. And dinner offers another opportunity for you to ensure that your child gets a healthy meal. A healthy dinner doesn't need to be elaborate or fancy. Basic healthy food can be easy and inexpensive to prepare.

Let's start with snacks before dinner. Children get hungry often, so make the snacks count. Cut-up raw vegetables with ranch dressing make a great snack before dinner. So, if your children turn their noses up at the cooked vegetables you make for dinner, at least you know they got some vitamins before the meal started. Adolescents tend to be lazy. If you do the preparation work of cutting up fruit or vegetables and make them easily accessible, kids will probably eat it.

Get your children involved in the process of planning dinners and preparing them. Lots of kids like to be in the kitchen and will be more likely to eat something they had a hand in creating. Some families take turns planning and cooking the meals. Give your child the responsibility of planning dinner once a week. You may be amazed with what he or she comes up with. Time spent in the kitchen preparing food also offers another opportunity to connect with your children and discuss what is on their minds, not to mention helping them learn a great life skill in how to prepare healthy food for themselves when they are on their own.

When trying to plan healthy dinners for preteens, you don't have to go for the leafy greens or cauliflower. Just keep it simple. Cheeseburgers and pasta salad with veggies mixed in can be a fast and easy dinner. Turkey meatballs and spaghetti is another easy favorite. Throw a little spinach into the sauce and you have a healthy dinner. A fun idea is making personal pizzas for dinner. Pizza is actually not a bad choice for a healthy dinner, and individual-size Boboli pizza crusts make this menu really easy. This way everyone can make his/her own. Breakfast for dinner is always a fun way to mix things up while still keeping it simple. Eggs, pancakes and French toast are all easy, fast and fairly nutritious. Even fruit with yogurt and toast can be a quick, light and healthy meal. And with no cooking.

If your family has managed to sit down to eat dinner together, there is something more important to discuss than the menu. A family dinner is a time to reconnect with one another. Many families don't have the opportunity to sit down and eat together every night, so when you do, make the most of it. Because families have busy schedules, if a family all sits down together for dinner, the conversation often turns to a recent issue parents have been wanting to discuss, such as the household chores that aren't being attended to or a poor report card that was received.

Please don't make the dinner table a battle ground. You want your children to enjoy having dinner as a family as much as you do. This isn't the time to discuss difficult issues or conflicts. Family dinners are sacred, so dinner conversation should be positive and fun. It is all about connection, not taking care of parenting business.

I have worked with parents who tell me that their preteens often complain of stomachaches during dinner and ask to leave the table early. So what is being discussed at dinner? Is it conversation that would make your stomach turn sour as well? Don't miss the opportunity to just be with your children, enjoying a meal, laughing, playing a game or having fun. Parenting business can be taken care of at another time. Keeping your relationship and open lines of communication with your children is so much more important.

The main point here is to keep your children's nutritional needs in perspective when they reach the interesting age of adolescence. There are so many other issues to deal with that I recommend keeping your child's diet as healthy as you can without making both you and your child crazy.

Hygiene

When it comes to hygiene, adolescents seem to go to extremes. Some children have the issue of not wanting to take care of themselves at all; others won't stop looking at themselves in the mirror. Both scenarios are normal and further illustrate what a confusing time adolescence can be.

For the parents who can't get their kids out of the bathroom, realize that this new- found interest in how they look is all part of trying to understand the new body image they are developing. It is important to respect this process and not make fun of their efforts to look a certain way or their extreme concern about their looks. This may cause some conflict in your home, depending on the ratio of bathrooms to people. If bathroom time becomes an issue in your home, try setting up an alternative area that can be used for extended primping time. Maybe it means setting up a vanity table and mirror in your child's bedroom or on a stairway landing. This can eliminate arguments over whose turn it is to use the bathroom and how long each person is taking to get ready in the morning. I made this suggestion to the mother of an eighth-grade girl. She installed a $10 full-length mirror on the back of her daughter's bedroom door. For very little money and effort, this solved the bathroom issue in their home. Solutions like these may be worthwhile as this issue could continue into your children's high school years.

The need for adolescents to look good goes beyond doing their hair over and over in the mirror. Most kids this age have a great deal of internal conflict as to what they should wear, what their skin looks like, whether they are over- or underweight. It is a time when children begin scrutinizing every part of themselves and comparing themselves to others. When your child begins this process, you may notice some odd behavior. Your children may ask you some bizarre questions or make strange requests. They may want to go to a doctor to treat their skin acne or want to get contacts to replace their glasses. Your child may ask what you and your spouse looked like at their age and what types of features such as noses are common in your family history. They will most likely take an interest in picking out their own clothes. I will never forget the best birthday gift I got when I was in middle school. My grandmother offered to take me shopping for an afternoon and let me pick out an outfit. It was a wonderful gift, as I felt special getting time alone with my grandmother and could pick out my own clothes. I realize as parents we have to put limits on things like choosing clothes, but try to be open within reason to what your children want to wear and what they think they look good in. Decision making is a great life skill that requires practice. Picking out clothes is a safe way to practice this important life skill.

Be empathetic with their struggle. It may seem silly to watch your child agonize over which pair of blue jeans to wear on the first day of school. Yet this is a true conflict for them and shouldn't be trivialized. Help your children showcase their best features and enhance their weaker ones. The best thing you can do is be supportive and understanding to what your children are experiencing. Share experiences from your own life to show your children that you truly understand their struggle. This isn't an easy part of turning into a teenager, but they will get through the dreaded awkward stage.

Some children have the opposite issue when entering adolescence. They are fearful and worried about the changes going on in their bodies, so they begin to regress to acting more childlike with the hopes of stopping this uncomfortable process. Of course, this doesn't work and acting younger won't stop the maturing process, but this is a way for children to seek some safety and security in a newly confused world.

Remember that adolescence is all about the struggle between wanting to continue being a carefree child and becoming an independent adult. In a lunch club that I ran for sixth-grade girls, the conversation would jump from playing with horses and Barbie dolls to why they weren't able to vote in the upcoming presidential election. I don't mean to imply that young women who play with horses and dolls shouldn't have a say in who is elected president, but it gives some insight into the jumps in their thinking and the conflict in making the leap into adulthood.

Some children have more difficulty taking this leap than others. Some kids continue with the hygiene habits that they used when younger, yet now that they have reached puberty this doesn't work anymore. There are kids in middle school who don't want to shower or bathe daily. They want to wear the same shirt for a number of days in a row and don't want to bother with fixing their hair or take special care of their skin. As puberty progresses, this becomes an issue as children start developing body odors, increased production of their sweat glands, and greasy hair and skin. At times, parents are in denial that their children are growing up and need to care of themselves differently than when they were younger. One problem is that middle-school kids can be ruthless and will make fun of a child who doesn't adopt new hygiene practices as they mature.

I once got a call from a sixth-grade teacher who was very concerned about a girl in her class. This girl was coming to school in dirty clothes and was beginning to have some body odor. The teacher noticed that other students were starting to talk about this girl's condition behind her back. I met with this girl to see whether there was something I could do to help. My main concern was that other students would start teasing her and would exaggerate any issue she might be having. Given the sensitive nature of this discussion, I spoke to her about the different adjustments that go along with starting middle school and wanted to make sure she was feeling comfortable this new school. Her body language said it all. She was quiet and shy and wanted to give the outward impression that everything was fine. I decided to talk to her parents, as this child was starting to do poorly in school and seemed to be regressing socially as well. Her mother was very defensive and angry with my suggestions that her daughter might have an adjustment issue to middle school and that it was affecting her personal hygiene. She felt that her daughter's appearance was fine and that I should mind my own business. I was initially discouraged, as I could understand how the mother felt but didn't want the daughter to suffer because of her mom's denial. But the very next day, the young girl showed up for school in clean clothes, her hair brushed and a smile on her face. Over time her teacher and I started seeing great progress from this student, academically and socially. There are often difficult issues with our children that we don't want to face, but they are important to address. If these issues aren't taken care of at home, I guarantee another student at school will notice. Middle-school students are not known for their tact or helpfulness when someone is having a personal problem. They are quick to tease and make fun. Addressing a personal issue comes much better from a caring parent than a teasing peer.

Exercise

Exercise is like most things, in that if you incorporate it into your regular life your children will incorporate it into theirs. If your family takes regular walks after dinner or spends weekends exploring the outdoors, your children will most likely continue these activities as they grow into adults. The only problem is that the hormonal changes that go on during adolescence make many children feel lazy. They don't want to go to sleep at night, yet are so tired they can't get up in the morning.

These feelings of laziness and being tired can make your children unmotivated to participate in any form of exercise. Yet exercise is so important for kids of this age, not only for the obvious health reasons but also as a way to blow off some of the steam that builds up with the frustration adolescence brings. Exercise can also be a lot of fun that may be a welcome change from the stress of life in middle school.

The best thing you can do is be a good role model for your children in the area of exercise. Plan family activities in which some exercise is required. A game of Frisbee on the beach or at a park can be a great way to slip in some exercise without your kids' realizing. Take turns picking family activities. Your kids may laugh when you pick ice skating or a night of bowling, but let down your hair and have some fun and most likely they will, too. Middle-school students like to engage in friendly competition. You might want to try participating in local walking or running events to raise money for local charities. The energy at a large organized event is contagious, and it may be the motivation that your child needs to participate. I suggest not talking a lot about doing these types of activities; just do them. The less you talk about it, the less chance your child has to tell you what a terrible idea that is. Just do it and see how they respond.

Remember to make it enjoyable for your kids. Exercise doesn't have to be regimented hard work. It can be light-hearted and fun. Think of activities that have some enjoyable element for a middle-school student. Possibly allow your child to bring a friend along. Friends are a top priority for middle-school students, so this may help them want to participate. Parents have also told me that, at times, bringing a friend along can offer a positive outlook on a certain activity. If your child sees that his friend likes the activity your family has chosen, then your child may become more engaged.

Be creative and don't give up. If a certain activity doesn't work, then try another one next time. Also, don't underestimate the power of bribery. Make sure the activity you choose includes an enticing carrot at the end. For instance, maybe a night of ice skating at the local rink will end with 30 minutes in the arcade. If you choose the activity, then maybe your child can choose the restaurant where you have dinner afterward.

Kids tend to start losing their playfulness and spontaneity during adolescence. Exercising and being active can help to revive those feelings. There seems to be so much pressure to grow up quickly in today's society. Exercise can be fun and remind children that it's OK at times just to act like kids, rather than rushing to become adults.

Sleep

Recent studies have revealed that a large majority of adolescents and teenagers are not getting enough sleep. According to the National Sleep Foundation, kids in this age group need 9-10 hours of sleep per night, and many aren't getting it. The consequences of not getting enough sleep can be great. Children often have difficulty in school, experience mood swings, and can get sick easily. The other concern is that they can develop delayed sleep phase syndrome. This is a condition in which kids have lots of energy late at night yet have trouble getting up in time for school and staying awake in their afternoon classes.

The two main reasons adolescents don't get enough sleep is that their parents leave it up to them to manage their sleep schedules and they get over-stimulated at night. Sleep needs to be a priority for you because your kids won't do it for themselves. If your children aren't getting enough sleep or if they're having sleep-related issues, here are a few things you can try.

The first step is to set a consistent bedtime that you enforce each night. Of course you can be more flexible on the weekends and during the summer, but when first instituting a new bedtime routine, be very consistent for at least a week so that your child's body can get used to the new pattern. If bedtime has gotten late over the summer, begin setting bedtime 15 minutes earlier each night until you get to the desired bedtime. Then enforce the desired bedtime for a week before school begins. This way, your son or daughter will be well rested to start the new school year and the beginning of a good sleep habit.

Turn off the TV, computer and/or video games at least an hour before bedtime. These activities are very stimulating and can prevent your child from being able to fall asleep easily or stay sound asleep throughout the night. This may mean that there isn't time for screens during the school week, but that's not such a bad thing, right? Encourage your child to have a winding-down period before bedtime. Taking a hot shower or bath, reading a book and drawing are examples of quieting activities that can be done before bed to help prepare your child for a good night's sleep.

Last, make sure your child doesn't eat or drink any caffeine after 4 p.m. Eating chocolate or drinking soda can make it difficult for your child to fall asleep at bedtime. If you feel your children are extremely sensitive to caffeine, you may want to cut it out of their diet completely.

Chapter 5

Peers

U p until adolescence, children are mostly influenced by their parents or whoever is their primary care giver. Your children watch every move you make and listen closely to everything you say. They may not always behave the way you would like, but you are the number one influence in their lives. They model their behavior after yours. This changes when children enter middle school. Middle-school students adopt their peers' behavior.

All of a sudden, your children become more concerned with what their friends think rather than opinions of their parents. Getting approval from their friends becomes their first priority. We all want to feel loved and accepted, and in middle school the ultimate goal is to have that acceptance from your peers. Unfortunately, most kids at this age don't have the self-confidence to demand acceptance from their peers, so they spend a lot of time and energy trying to become what they think is acceptable within their peer group. This becomes their top priority over most other areas of life. Adolescents will give up or change their lives dramatically to fit in. They have been known to drop certain friends, try to make new friends, dress differently, act differently, listen to new music, eat new foods, use new words to express themselves and more, just because they think that is what their peers expect.

Parents often have difficulty relating to their children while these changes are taking place. First of all, these changes can catch parents by surprise if they aren't mentally prepared for this switch in priorities. Secondly, kids often morph into something new that even their own parents don't recognize. Don't worry too much. Your child is going through a transition, but he is still the same child you raised deep down inside. He may look a lot different on the outside, but he continues to possess the same value system you have instilled over the years.

So what is this obsession and new importance placed on peers? This is the beginning of the self-actualization process. This is the process in which kids begin seeing themselves as adults and seeing their parents as real people. Parents, after all, are human and aren't perfect. This is when our children begin making that realization. This is the time when your children begin pulling away from you and turning toward their peers, which is all part of growing up.

At times I have met parents who are in denial about their children's growing up and try to pretend that they aren't going through this process. I understand that this change is difficult to comprehend; yet if your goal as a parent is to help your children become self-reliant adults, then you must help them through this process. Pretending that this isn't happening will only make things worse.

On the other hand, some parents decide to let go when their children begin pulling away from them and moving toward their friends. They don't fight the process but rather give in and allow their children more freedom and independence than they can handle. This isn't a good approach, either. I encourage you to work toward finding a happy medium.

Keep in mind that even though children see their friends as important influences in their lives, it is still your job to decide what is best for your child and your family. This is not a time to give up your parental power. The decisions you make may not always be popular, but that is your job.

Communication

Keeping up with one's peers is no easy task, so most middle-school students find it necessary to be in constant communication with their friends. This issue seems to affect girls in middle school more than boys, but families of middle-school boys will definitely begin noticing the interest in cell phones, texting, online social media, etc.

Communication in middle school tends to be of the "he said, she said" nature: "Jenny told me that you don't like my new jacket, but when we were at the mall you told me you loved it and wanted one just like it," and it goes on from there. Kids tend to say things that they think their friends want to hear rather than what they really think. Multiply this problem over a group of seventh-grade girls and you have got a tangled web of details that can make or break any one of them.

A huge part of the communication process in middle school includes rumors. No one spreads rumors on purpose (or so they say), but if everyone is talking about everyone else, stories will spread and the details may get exaggerated and confused through the process. Remember the game of Telephone or Gossip? The last one in the circle always hears something completely different from what was originally said. This is life on a middle-school campus.

The good news about rumors is that no single rumor stays popular for too long. There are so many rumors flying around about so many people that if one starts about your child, you can assure her it will blow over soon. The bad news about rumors is that they can be very hurtful. When a child has been the victim of a rumor at school or online, it is a good opportunity to assess current friendships and decide whether these are the people he or she really wants to be associated with.

The best defense against rumors is to be as honest as possible and for kids to stick to their own business as best they can. The trouble begins when kids try to enter into other people's business. Although it may seem like fun at first, this can backfire easily.

Parents often find it difficult to communicate with their children when they enter adolescence. Part of the problem is that many adolescents choose not to share much with their parents. Please don't take this personally; it isn't meant to hurt you. Middle-school students spend much more time and energy communicating with their friends. So much that they often develop their own language.

Currently there are a few different teen languages being used on e-mail and cell phones. I am sure you can remember some words or sayings that you used with your friends when you were this age. In an effort to communicate better with their children, some parents attempt to learn and use this secret language of their children and their peers. This is a commendable effort but may not be welcomed. I would recommend that, as parents, you keep your ears and eyes open and be aware of these languages, but don't attempt to use them with your child. Moreover, keep tabs on what is going on in a less obvious way but continue to model standard communication methods with your child. Eventually they will grow out of using their teen talk and will then have been exposed to good communications skills when they are ready to use them.

The bottom line: It is OK for your child to have a special way of communicating with friends, but just make sure you stay present and involved so that communication with peers doesn't replace experiences with your family and your family's values.

Everyone in middle school wants to be well liked and popular. The reality is that not everyone will become popular, so try to encourage your children to foster good friendships and be honest and true to themselves. If they take that approach, they will have a good chance of avoiding the rumor mill.

Be understanding of your child's need to talk to or e-mail his/her friends constantly. At the same time, it is your job to set limits on this communication that work for you and your family. I recommend setting a certain time of the day in which your children can talk on the phone or e-mail with friends. Anytime outside of that, they will need to ask for special permission from you or wait until the next day to talk to their friends at school.

It is very important that you find a way to supervise the use of cell phones and online communication tools that your kids are using. One suggestion is to have everyone check their cell phones at the door when coming into the house. Keep a box, small table or some sort of container near the front entrance of the house in which everyone puts their cell phone in when they are at home. I also strongly discourage parents from allowing kids to have computers in their rooms. Keep the computer in a family-centered part of your home, not your children's bedrooms.

Even in today's high-technology world, using a cell phone or a computer is a privilege that you have allowed your child, but if that privilege isn't being used appropriately, you may need to take it away. It is a lot easier to do this if you have established good rules for where these devices live and how and when they are to be used. Secondly, children of this age need a lot of supervision. If your child is talking on a cell phone, texting or chatting online in the bedroom, it will be difficult for you to supervise. And lastly, talking on the phone or using the computer late at night can interrupt your child's sleep, so it is important that you can easily enforce limits for usage.

Conflicts

As a school counselor, much of my time is spent helping students resolve conflicts. Many of these conflicts are with other students. Adolescence is a confusing time, so it is no wonder that conflicts arise among students. Middle-school girls and boys handle conflicts very differently. When boys get upset with one another, they may get into a scuffle on the playground, get sent to the office and by the time they sit down with an administrator, the conflict is over. They get mad, get their aggression out and then move on. Schools often come down hard on this behavior because of the physical nature of how boys handle these arguments. Boys will often get punished for something that they are completely over already.

Girls, on the other hand, hold onto everything. I once sat down with a group of sixth-grade girls who were having a difficult time getting along and asked one of them when this conflict began. She told me a story that went back to the first day of school in the second grade. These girls had been carrying the same conflict around for four years! When girls get in arguments with one another, they can be very nasty verbally, but it rarely gets physical.

Girls make threats, write mean notes, call one another names and get friends to turn against other friends. Until recently, schools haven't had a formal process to handle these types of arguments, unlike an argument that ends up in a physical confrontation. Yet in light of recent news of how damaging these types of conflicts can be to children, schools are beginning to come down harder on them. Schools are also implementing programs and activities like peer-to-peer conflict resolution programs to bring awareness of conflicts to the students as well as teach them skills to handle these situations. But again, with budget cuts and less staff available in schools, these types of programs tend to be the first to go.

Bullying

Much of this behavior could be put under the category of bullying. Bullying has long been a problem in middle schools because the environment is one in which everyone is feeling unsure of himself and seeking approval from peers. This dynamic will commonly cause someone who feels inferior to become condescending or look down upon another student who is perceived to be weaker. They then become bullies as a way of making themselves feel less inferior. This dynamic is destructive, especially to the kids perceived as weaker. Lots of kids in middle school have poor self-esteem, and being bullied by others only makes this problem worse.

Until recently, schools generally took a light stand on the issue of bullying, as it was considered "typical kid stuff." The bloodshed at Columbine High School was an eye-opening experience for the education system as well as parents as it revealed the tragic consequences of bullying. If your child is bullying others, you need to realize this is a sign that he feels bad about himself. Parents can help their children improve their self-image by consistently being accepting and caring for them at home. Help them find activities either within or outside of school in which they feel comfortable and accepted among their peers. Encourage them to develop relationships with kids they trust, even if it is just one or two. There is no reason kids need to have a big group of friends. Some kids will always feel more comfortable having one or two close friends rather than a large group. Most importantly, help them understand their worth and importance in this world and that their purpose is much greater than making others feel worse about themselves.

If your child is a victim of bullying, try to understand that he may also have a very poor self-image. Children need caring and acceptance from their families. They need support to build them up in their areas of interest. It is important to help your children realize their potential while being realistic about their shortcomings and how to compensate for them. There is a trick to dealing with bullies. It is called "fake it until you make it." If you can teach your child to pretend that the bully's comments don't bother him, then the bully will eventually stop picking on your child, as it won't be fun. He won't be able to upset your child or get the desired reaction. Now this is hard to do, as the bully's comments may really hurt your child's feelings. So practice. You can role-play these situations with your child at home and let him practice different reactions so that he is prepared when that bully strikes again. By the way, this strategy works with adult bullies, too, so don't hesitate to try it out if you are experiencing an adult bully at work or in your social circle. After all, some of these adult bullies have been getting away with this a long time and need to be stopped.

SO

One of the best ways to defuse someone who is teasing or being a bully is to show them you don't care (even if you do). And it only takes one word 'So'. When the bully says something mean like 'Your so ugly' all your child has to say is 'So' with attitude and then walk away. The bully will be embarrassed and frustrated that he/she didn't get a desired reaction and that may be the end of the program. If your child is being teased, practice this with them at home and then have them give it a try.

Schools are taking bullying very seriously these days, and so should parents. Children deserve a safe, friendly environment in which the emphasis is on learning, not survival. Schools have made great strides in creating this environment for our children, yet there is still work to be done. As parents, we must be advocates for our children. It is our job to bring these situations to the school's attention if that hasn't already taken place. I also encourage you to work with parents of children who are causing problems for your child. These parents may not be aware of the situation, and the two families may be able to work out these issues together.

The most important thing is to take bullying seriously, regardless of which side of the conflict your child is on. It is a damaging process for all children involved. The earlier we can deal with issues of bullying, the sooner our children will begin using these valuable life lessons. Having strong self-images and standing up for themselves in a positive way are two skills that will serve your children well as they become adults.

Chapter 6

Parenting and home life

H ome life with children in middle school is much different from when they were younger. These changes cause us to rethink how we make plans for our middle-school children and how we structure home life. First off, I challenge all parents not to tackle this job alone. Raising a family isn't easy today, and we all need help. Many parents that I talk to get so busy with the details of everyday life that they don't take the time and step back to see how they could manage things differently. The Rambo approach of pulling out your guns and doing it yourself works, but there are costs. The costs are your health and sanity, two very important components in continuing to be a good parent. So take care of yourself and get some help. Reading this book is a really good first step.

Extended Family and Friends

Remember when you brought your new baby home from the hospital. Friends and family alike asking, "What can we do to help?" Neighbors showing up with pre-cooked dinners and gifts of kindness showing up in so many unexpected ways. Well, as you know, those days are over. But that doesn't mean the people close to you and your family aren't able and willing to help out. Most people just don't ask. In addition to helping you with your parental responsibilities, there is a second advantage to getting extended family members and friends to assist you with your children. Your children will benefit greatly from having other adult relationships, particularly with adults whom you trust to have value systems similar to your own.

It is amazing how children of all ages act so differently with adults other than their parents. They are often on their best behavior and show a lot of respect for the authority of other adults. Respect is a concept that middle-school students are naturally questioning, so giving them an opportunity to be respectful of other adults is a wonderful life lesson.

On the other hand, when asking extended family members to be with your children, it is important not to wear out their welcome. It is also important to be realistic about your extended family's ability to be good caregivers. For example, I don't recommend using grandparents as everyday, after-school caregivers unless you have a very special situation. Many times these care-giving arrangements can come with resentment, which doesn't create the best environment for your child. Some, but not all, grandparents are interested in, and capable of providing a very positive after-school environment for their grandkids. Maybe a situation such as Grandpa spending Sunday mornings taking your son to the driving range or an aunt taking your daughter for a day of shopping before a special birthday is more feasible for your family.

Family friends also can be a wonderful resource for help. Especially if they also have children so you can possibly create a give-and-take situation to help one another. Again, this is something we often do when our children our small. We share babysitting, carpooling, etc. When children start middle school, parents tend to not see one another as often and therefore don't build close relationships in which they feel comfortable asking one another for help. It may take more effort to build these relationships, but your time and effort will pay off. Again there are more advantages than just getting some help with your parental responsibilities. It is very important to get to know the parents of your children's friends. We will discuss that more in the section on supervision, but as friends become a driving force in your children's lives, it is helpful to have already built relationships with their families.

Remembering your childhood

When I work with students who are struggling in middle school, I share with them some of my own experiences during this time in my life. I share how awkward and fat I felt. How I never seemed to have the right clothes at the right time. How I could never get my hair to look like Farah Fawcett's when it seemed that everyone else could. I share stories such as the time I got a new pair of Levi 501 button-fly jeans to wear to a school dance. The only problem was that when you first buy these jeans, they are very dark blue and stiff as a board. The cool thing was to wash them to death and wear them very worn-looking. But I had only two days to get them soft and worn-looking to wear to the dance. So I washed my new jeans as many times as I could over those two days and wore them to the dance slightly damp, as I didn't have time to dry them thoroughly on the day of the dance. I share how I really wanted my jeans to be just right for the dance but nothing ever seemed quite right during those days.

But I always end these stories with the good news—life in middle school is so difficult that it can only get better from here. That is exactly what happened for me, and I try to help middle-school students see that life will get better for them as well. My hope is that they will feel comfortable in their own skin soon and when they do, they will have what they need to face the challenges that life brings.

Children need this type of hope and encouragement through their pre-teen years. They need to know that you have had struggles in your life and that they will feel better about themselves at some point. The problem is, some kids are just not that pleasant to be around during this time in their lives, and many students of middle-school age don't want to talk a whole lot, especially to their parents.

But this is an excellent opportunity for you to dig into your memory banks and put yourself back in the shoes of someone attending middle school each day. Look back at pictures of yourself and see what your reaction is now to how you looked during that time. Ask yourself what you liked to do during middle school and what was important to you. Whom did you like to spend time with, and what did you enjoy doing? What do you remember from school? Do any teachers or classes stick out in your memory? Even if you don't have the opportunity to share these experiences with your child, having empathy for what he or she is going through will go a long way in continuing to be a giving parent during this phase of development.

Middle-school students don't share every detail of their daily lives readily, but they do want to talk and to be heard, most importantly by their parents. If you stay open and don't try forcing your children to share with you, they will in their own way. The tricky part is being willing to listen when they want to talk. Of course they will pick the most inopportune time to share their innermost thoughts and ideas with you. It will be when you are rushing to an important meeting or while you are on the phone dealing with something difficult and detailed. Adolescents are not known for their timing, but I encourage you to make their needs the priority when they ask for your attention. I believe that adolescents unconsciously choose times to talk to you when they know you are busy. This approach is a way of affirming your love for them, and they are putting you to the test. I know it is difficult, but if at all possible, drop what you are doing and give them your undivided attention. If you don't, you may lose a valuable opportunity to find out what is really going on with your children as well as an opportunity to share or teach them something worthwhile. If you don't make yourself available when they ask, you are sending a message that their needs are not a priority to you, and they may not come to you again.

Parenting styles

Have you ever heard something come out of your mouth and feel as if you are channeling your mother or father? People always say they will never act like their parents, but the reality is that this relationship is our main influence growing up so it is almost impossible to separate ourselves completely from the actions of the people who raised us. Then there are those adults who hated the way they were raised, so they choose a parenting style that is the polar opposite from their own parents' style. This can have consequences as well in that parenting is a balancing act, not an extreme sport. If you are trying so hard to do things differently from someone else, some parents end up over-compensating and using a parenting style that may not be effective or give them the results they desire.

Whatever parenting style you have developed, your child knows it well by the time he or she is old enough to go to middle school. Some parents are fearful of this age group and feel they need to change their parenting style to be more strict or rigid with their children when they reach middle school. Unfortunately, this approach rarely works, as your parenting style has developed over the years in a natural way. Your style is most likely a combination of what you learned from your parents (for better or worse) combined with your own life experiences, as well as accommodating for your child's temperament. No matter what your style is, if you try to change it drastically, it will seem forced and your child will see right through you. With that said, there is no reason you can't modify your parenting style and choose to do things differently. I just don't recommend trying to completely change your style at this point in your or your children's lives.

I worked with a mother who used a passive parenting style as her children were going through elementary school. She would let them do whatever they wanted unless there was extreme danger involved. This mother set very few limits for her children. She felt that her children naturally knew what they needed so she would follow their lead. This approach seemed to work fine until her children got to middle school and high school. At that point their behavior made her very nervous. All of a sudden, she realized that her children's natural urges were not in line with the way she felt they should behave. So she read a book about an authoritarian style of parenting and decided to change the way things were going in her home. She suddenly administered very strict rules and restrictions on her children. She implemented extreme limits to the point that her children felt they were being punished for everything. This mother also interpreted this style of parenting as one in which you couldn't show your children love during this process as you would come across as being weak and not in control. As you can imagine, this extreme change in parenting style did not bring the results this mother was looking for. At first, her children were distraught and shocked by this new parenting style their mother had adopted. After getting over the initial shock, the children began to lie and find ways to sneak around their mother's new rules and restrictions. And maybe worst of all, they didn't feel that they could go to their mother for support or help, so they turned to their friends to fulfill these needs instead.

The main message is that you will need to adapt your parenting style as your children grow and change. But there is no need to attempt to completely change your parenting style, especially if you are attempting to change to a style that is drastically different from your own family values and/or personality. It is more important to continue seeking parenting support and education as your children mature and to always use your own best judgment as to how to incorporate those new ideas into your own family structure.

Supervision

When children reach middle school, many parents feel a great sense of accomplishment that their son or daughter is so much more mature now and able to handle more responsibilities. That may be true, but this is also an age when children need to be given more responsibility in a highly structured environment. This is definitely not a time to rest on your laurels as parents in any way. Many parents do, and this is a big mistake.

Middle school encompasses the in-between years when kids don't really need a baby-sitter yet are really too young to stay alone unsupervised. This often becomes an issue for working parents. Unfortunately it isn't safe to let your children be out in the neighborhood unsupervised, so most parents tell their kids that they have to stay at home alone. This can cause children to be very lonely and bored. Loneliness and boredom can lead to unwanted behavior, so this is definitely not a good idea. It takes some creativity and effort to arrange for after-school activities for middle-school students, but the investment is definitely worthwhile.

Some, but unfortunately not all, schools offer some sort of after-school program on their campuses. If your school district does offer something, look into it even if your child resists. The local park and recreation departments or the local police often run these programs. Both of these organizations receive grants to provide after-school programs as an effort to prevent high-risk behavior among kids of this age group. Keeping middle-school children in a positive, supervised activity after school is a well-known challenge, so a number of organizations try to offer solutions. Because many of these programs are grant-funded, there are often scholarships available. Don't be afraid to ask.

Extracurricular activities can also be a great way of providing supervised care for your children while they are getting the benefits from the program. Whether it is in sports, music, art or a social group, keeping your children involved is a wonderful way to keep them on a positive track during this difficult time in growing up. It will take a little effort on your part to research these activities and possibly work with other parents to make arrangements to get your children to and from these programs. But again, the time and effort will pay back on many levels.

Keeping your children busy and safe after school can be an excellent opportunity for you to team up with other parents and work together on a solution for this problem. Maybe each parent takes off work early one day a week and keeps the kids at their house or is the one in charge of driving them around to after-school activities. This may be a time to call on the help of your extended family members. Retired grandparents are great at taking kids to after-school sports practice or to the library to start on their homework.

Additionally, employers are becoming more realistic about the need to offer a flexible work schedule. Give some thought to how your hours at work could be rearranged so that you are able to be home from 3 to 6 p.m. Maybe you could start your day earlier and end early. Or maybe you could stagger your work schedule with your spouse's so that one of you is home when your child arrives. Middle-school students are most at risk during those after-school hours, so do what you can to make sure your children have good, safe supervision during that time.

Some middle-school students will protest against setting up after-school supervision for them. They may want to stay home alone after school even if it isn't the safest way to go. This is one of the many situations as parents where we know best and our decision may not be popular with our kids, but we have to do it anyway. Providing supervision for your child isn't about being popular. It is about doing what you know is best for your child, even if he or she doesn't agree.

Divorce

Obviously, all family circumstances are different, but from my experience and research, there is a trend in how children manage divorce when they enter adolescence. It doesn't seem to matter how old your children are when you got divorced, adolescence is a new developmental phase and children with divorced parents often go through a readjustment between the ages of 11 and 14 regardless of how old they were when their parents actually divorced.

Adolescence is the time when children begin seeing themselves in adult relationships. This is just the beginning of a process that takes quite a while, but children begin to see their parents in a new way and often gain some new perspective on their parents' relationship. This can bring lots of new feelings, as well as resurrect some old ones regarding your divorce. These feelings often catch parents off guard, especially if they have been divorced for a long time. They have made the necessary adjustments and have since gone on with their lives. But children handle divorce much differently than parents, and most children of divorced families go through another adjustment somewhere between ages 11 and 14.

My parents divorced when I was 11 years old. Up until that time, my parents could do no wrong in my eyes. As I entered adolescence, I started to see my parents as regular human beings rather than the all-knowing, all-doing parents I had depended on for everything. I didn't understand the choices my parents were making. I became angry and frustrated with my father and grew up too fast to try to help my mother. When I reached my late 20s, I clearly had a problem in my personal life. I was afraid of commitment in a relationship and assumed that no one would ever commit to being with me. Unconsciously, I was so convinced that every man was going to leave me that they did. Of course it was my wise mother who pointed out this problem to me. She knew that I wouldn't be able to have a healthy, long-term, committed relationship with a man until I came to terms with the abandonment I had felt when my parents divorced. She was right, and because of her, my story has a happy ending. I am happily married and have a nice relationship with both of my parents. I attribute the success of my story mostly to the wisdom and strength of my mother. I wish the same for your children.

So what does this mean to you, a divorced parent raising a child during these adolescent years? It means that the decisions you are making greatly affect your children's lives now and for the future. I don't mean to say you should stay in a bad relationship for the sake of your children. I mean that there are ways to separate from your partner and still help your children feel wanted, loved and secure. It also means that the more honest and loving you can be to your children, regardless of the difficult times you may be experiencing, the better. It also means that you may be forced to reopen a door to the feelings and issues from your divorce even if it occurred a number of years ago. Your child may need your help to assess his or her own feelings about that rift now that he or she is an adolescent and seeing these events in a different way.

Here are a few tips and recommendations for divorced families with children in middle school.

One home

Find a way for your child to live in the same home all the time. Adolescence is a rocky time for children. There is a lot of change and uncertainty going on in their bodies and minds. Now more than ever, they need the stability of sleeping in the same bed, in the same home every night. Environment and personal possessions become very important to middle-school students. Feeling connected with their friends is crucial. Consistency of house rules is vital. For these basic reasons and many others, I highly recommend that children live with one parent and spend time with the other. I recommend children spending lots of time with both parents but living primarily in one place.

Shared Custody

I worked with a family where the parents divorced and had one son who had just entered the sixth grade. I was asked to work with this boy, as he was falling behind in his school work. When I met him for the first time, I noticed he had a backpack almost as big as he was. I offered to put it down in my office and came to find that his backpack was extremely heavy. So jokingly, I asked whether he was carrying his whole life in this backpack. He chuckled and said no but then explained that he was carrying all of his books and everything he would need for the next day, as he was spending the night at his dad's house. I then came to find out that this boy goes home to a different home every night. He alternates spending the night between his mom's and dad's houses each night. I couldn't believe that they really had such a hectic visitation agreement, so I called his parents to discuss this situation. Both of them confirmed that this was their visitation agreement and that they liked it this way. They both told me that they loved their son so much that they couldn't stand the thought of not seeing him at least every other day so they came up with this idea to have him change houses each night. I tried to show them how this was unsettling and very taxing on their son. I was completely unsuccessful in convincing them of any other living arrangement for their son. So we talked about ways of trying to help their son within this situation even though I strongly disagreed with them. When I was talking to the boy about his situation, he would just say that he knew it was crazy but he did it to keep his parents happy. Please don't make the mistake of making a living arrangement that your children accept primarily because they have no choice and secondarily to make you happy. I understand that people get divorced for valid reasons, but our children's needs still should come first.

I once worked with a woman who was divorced and had three children. She and her ex-husband kept their family home when they separated and then rented an apartment nearby. Instead of transferring the children from the house to the apartment and back, the parents took turns living in the house raising their children. This admittedly unusual arrangement took a lot of cooperation between the parents, but the results were very positive. They had three well-adjusted children who got the benefit of living with both the parents and didn't have to make any relocation adjustments from their own home. I understand that this type of arrangement isn't always possible, but it does illustrate that there are creative solutions. Please consider some sort of living arrangement that is in the best interests of our child.

One voice

Offer one voice to your children's school. Middle schools are very busy places dealing with hundreds of families each day. Your family will have a much better chance of getting what you want and need for your child if you make it easy for the school to communicate with you. I highly recommend both parents be active participants in a child's education. Both of you can be at parent/teacher conferences, attend parent meetings, join the PTA, volunteer on campus, etc. But when it comes to communicating with the school, make one parent the main point of contact. And then for all other decisions, be adults and work together for the sake of your children.

Kind words

Never speak unfavorably about your ex-partner in front of your children. I have discussed this issue with many parents who assure me that they are very careful not to say bad things about the other parent around the children. Yet when they become aware of this potential issue, they realize that they do this in subtle ways. A rolling of the eyes or comment under one's breath counts. Be careful. Your children are watching and listening even if you don't realize it.

In general, talking badly about your ex-partner is setting a poor example for your children, but the issue goes deeper than trying to instill good values. Kids see themselves as a part of you. If a parent speaks poorly about the other parent, children may feel that you think poorly of them as well.

You should also be aware of the more direct ways your comments can affect your children. My favorite one is, "You are just like your father (or mother)." This may be true, but if you say it in front of your kids, make sure it is referring to positive qualities.

I think this is one of the hardest things for parents, divorced or married. We all get annoyed and frustrated with our partners at times, so these comments just slip out. I also find that many parents don't have a good support system for themselves. Parenting is an exhausting job with very few breaks, yet we all need to take care of ourselves to be good parents. Your frustrations with your partner need to be handled in another way. Talk to a friend, take some time away from the family for yourself, get regular exercise. All of these are healthier ways of handling issues with your partner or ex-partner so that you can be the loving and giving parent when you are with your children.

Parenting is a selfless job. Being a divorced parent puts your selflessness to the ultimate test. Don't try to do it alone. Get the help and support you need so you can offer your kids the best part of you.

Home life

In my opinion we should scratch the word "chores" from our family vocabulary. It takes a lot of work to keep a family well taken care of, and everyone in the house shares that responsibility. Somehow the word "chore" has come to mean a way for parents to make children do tasks around the house just to be mean or as a way to justify giving kids money. It should be a given that everyone helps out in whatever way they are able. That way the whole family will have time and energy to have fun and lead well-balanced lives. Now back to reality.

Many families make the mistake of doing everything for their children until they get to be 10 or 11 years old. Once the children get to middle school, parents feel that they are old enough and able to handle the responsibility of helping around the house. Children of this age are definitely able to take on some household responsibilities, but if this is a new concept for your children, you may need to implement some sort of system to get started. This is also an age at which many children want to start having their own spending money, so they see helping around the house as a good way of making an income. Bad idea.

If you feel your kids need their own spending money, give it to them or help them get an age-appropriate job to earn some money. But don't use spending money as a carrot to lure your kids into pulling their weight around the house. It is very healthy for children to learn that they are an integral part of what makes their household run smoothly. Being part of a family means helping out on a regular basis. It should not be an option to offer doing extra tasks for Mom or Dad just to earn some extra money when you need it. This is wonderful life lesson that your future daughters- or sons-in-law will thank you for some day.

Since children at this age want to feel grown-up and are very concerned with fairness and purpose, choose your strategy for getting help around the house carefully. I often hear parents complain that their children don't help around the house. A common complaint about a middle-school-age son is, "The only thing we ask is that he take out the garbage once a week. That is all we ask, and he can't even do that."

Well, let's look at this strategy. First of all, you have given your child a responsibility that occurs weekly. It isn't realistic to expect an adolescent to remember to do something that occurs only once a week. Remembering a daily routine would be much more realistic, as it would become habitual. A weekly task is hard for many people to remember, especially children this age. Secondly, what message do you think you are sending when the most important thing that you ask of your child is to deal with the most awful thing in your house, the garbage?

Children need to feel important, so put them in charge of an important aspect of running your home. Kids of this age are capable of handling all sorts of household duties. They can make meals, do dishes, mow the lawn, do laundry, dust and vacuum. Training and guidance are a key part of making this type of strategy work, but in time I think you will be amazed at how much kids can do to take the entire household burden off you.

To implement a strategy of sharing the household responsibilities, I recommend starting off with a family meeting. Family meetings are a useful tool that I recommend parents begin having on a regular basis. Here is one topic that is very well suited for the family meeting forum. Serving snacks is a good way to getting a family meeting off on the right foot. The snacks provide something enjoyable to offer a slight distraction from the business at hand but don't get in the way of taking care of business. Ask to have a volunteer to be the family meeting recorder or secretary before you begin. This person is in charge of writing down the decisions made during the meeting. Give a brief explanation of why you have called this meeting and let it be known that you expect to end the meeting with a plan everyone agrees to. Then present a list of household responsibilities that need to be taken care of and on what schedule. Each item on the list should be accompanied by a detailed description of what you expect to be accomplished by the person in charge of that household duty. Of course there will be some responsibilities that parents must take care of, so make sure to mark those on the list before presenting it at the meeting. Then you can discuss who likes to do what. You can discuss options of switching responsibilities on a weekly or monthly basis. Be careful not to switch responsibilities too often, as it gets confusing as to who is in charge of what. Also, depending on the temperament of your children, they may get better and more efficient at a certain duty the longer they are responsible for doing it.

Continue the discussion until all items on the list have been accounted for. Be as open-minded as you can. Your children may offer some good suggestions of how to do things differently. Be willing to try something new for a short period of time. The end result of your meeting should be a plan of who is going to do what and for how long.

Your children may ask what the consequence is if they don't do a certain task on their list of responsibilities. In most cases there will be a natural consequence that you could reference. For instance, if you don't make dinner for the family, then everyone (including yourself) will go hungry. But if it isn't that cut and dried, have a discussion of how the household won't run smoothly if everyone doesn't pull their weight. Once you implement this plan, each family member is responsible for checking off their duties as they do them. If someone isn't doing his or her tasks, I would recommend having that family member come up with a punishment or taking away something that the whole family enjoys to make the point that if one member doesn't pull his weight, the whole family suffers.

When children get to middle school, they tend to have more homework. Sometimes parents are reluctant to give kids a lot of responsibility at home as it may take away from their homework time. Keep in mind that kids of this age are much more efficient if kept busy. Problems tend to occur when they have too much unstructured time on their hands.

Dinner conversation

As you know, families keep very busy schedules. These schedules seem to get even more hectic when your children become middle-school-age. So when is family time? Most families I know make an attempt to have dinner together at least a couple of nights a week. This can be a wonderful experience for all involved. Dinner together is a great time to reconnect, share and have some fun. Yet most family dinners don't turn out that way. Because families don't spend a lot of time together, these dinners often turn into opportunities for parents to discuss important, yet not necessarily pleasant, matters with their children. Parents may want to talk about a recent report card or find out the progress of an upcoming school project. One parent may use this time as an opportunity to tell the other parent how the children weren't well behaved that day or didn't do their expected household duties. Kids may also use this opportunity to ask their parents a question that could cause a conflict, such as asking whether they could spend the night at a certain friend's house that weekend or whether they could have some money to buy the latest video game.

These types of discussions can turn a nice family gathering into an unhappy war zone very quickly. Families need to have discussions, and they need to talk about difficult topics as well as fun things. But if you are going make the effort to have family dinners, make the most of them. They can be a great time to check in on one another, play a game and remember how closely you are all connected and enjoy being together. Find other times to discuss the more difficult topics. Private discussions in a quiet setting are often better for addressing topics such as grades or enforcing curfew rules. I guarantee you will all have less indigestion and your children will welcome the opportunity to make it home for a family dinner rather than dreading the obligation.

Technology

If they haven't already, students entering middle school tend to develop a great interest in technology: computers, e-mail, chatting, Facebook, cell phones, video games, etc. Most middle-school students will develop a passion for two or three items on this list, yet all of these items can become a real issue in your home if not handled well.

First of all, I never recommend putting any sort of screen in a child's bedroom, computer or TV. As a parent it is your job to supervise and monitor the use of these things. If they are in a child's room behind closed doors, you have given up your control. Secondly, set rules of when and how these items can be used. Give your children certain times of the day that they can watch TV or use their cell phones. The rest of the time, turn off the computer, have a place to park the cell phones, and keep the noise of technology away from your family time. Additionally, set limits on how long they can do these activities and restrict their use until after other responsibilities such as homework or household duties have been taken care of. Lastly, supervise, supervise, supervise! The best way to keep your child from overusing and abusing of technology is to keep her busy in other positive activities. That way she truly won't have the time or energy to talk or text on the phone for hours or play video games until 2 a.m. I realize that technology is a big part of all of our lives, but feel it is still important to teach our children how to relate to people in person, not just through a screen or a keyboard.

Middle-school students are very tech-savvy these days. Of course they all tell their parents they are using the computer to do their homework, but there is a lot of time spent on the Internet and sending instant messages to friends. You should have a lot of concerns with your child having access to the Internet without your being present to supervise. Unfortunately, the Internet can be a way for people to hide their true identities and trick young people into thinking they are talking to a peer when they are really making friendships with adults purposely deceiving children. Sending e-mails to friends and using Instant Messenger is a fun way for young people to communicate with one another, but I have seen cases where it was misused and friends ended up getting hurt. Kids have been known to misrepresent themselves to others as a way of getting secret information from a peer. This is called cyber bullying and is more and more prevalent. Make sure to talk to your children about appropriate behavior when online and again, supervise!

There can also be more serious consequences in which these communications can be used as evidence in a court of law. Now you might ask yourself who would care about teenage chatter on the computer, but there have been situations in which students have committed crimes and then talked about it with friends on their computers. If your child gets involved in a conversation of this nature, he can become part of the legal case.

Even though our world has become very high-tech, don't forget potential issues with the old TV. There has been a lot in the media about the effects on children from watching too much TV and playing video games. I wouldn't take these studies lightly. The research and knowledge about the effects of TV and video games on our kids has only just begun. I believe that we will continue seeing information on how these activities are best kept to a minimum. One of the issues with TV is that it is information thrown out to viewers with little or no context around the content. My recommendation is that you limit the time your children watch TV and that you watch it with them or at least be present when they are watching. That way you have the opportunity to help your children understand why what they're watching is important and how it fits or doesn't fit into your family values. I also think that watching what your kids are interested in gives you some perspective into what they are thinking and feeling. Getting this perspective from kids of this age isn't easy, so you have to use back-door methods such as watching TV with them or going to movies that they want to see.

One issue with computer games is their often violent nature and the unnatural adrenalin rush kids get from playing them. I don't believe that a video game encourages a child to be violent unless he already has that tendency for another reason. But I do believe that these games can give kids a false sense of reality and a charge of energy that they don't always know what to do with. Again, limit their time spent on video games and make sure your children have a balance of activities that they enjoy doing. I realize that at times your child may feel some peer pressure to obtain a certain level of skill in a video game. If that is the case and you approve of the activity, help your child achieve that skill, but again offer a variety of life activities.

The use and knowledge of technology is not all bad. The world in which our children will be working as adults will demand their ability to learn new technology and seek knowledge in new areas. Using computers and playing video games is often the beginning of this learning for many children. Yet like anything in life, it is important to strike a balance in the activities your children engage in.

Chapter 7

Experimenting

E xperimentation is perhaps what parents fear most, as their
children become teenagers. We were all teenagers once and
we all experimented with different things. Remembering the risks
we took and looking back at how unsafe we were at times is enough
to make a parent of a middle-school-age child really nervous.

Some experiments are much more dangerous and serious than
others, but the reality is that experimenting and making mistakes
are part of growing up. So try not to fear this process but rather
work toward understanding it and offer the right type of support
for your child who is going through it.

Different approaches

Some parents feel that setting very strict limits and restrictions
for their children entering adolescence will prevent them from
experimenting. Don't fool yourself. You can't stop your children
from trying new things. It is in their genetic makeup to do so. But

you can make sure your children have a strong base of values that will give them good judgment to guide them through these trying times.

If you try to prevent them from doing anything out of your sight, you will most likely lead your children into lying and rebelling against you. That approach probably won't give you the desired results. You may want to consider another approach.

Trying something new

Sarah was an eighth-grader I worked with from the time she started middle school in the sixth grade. She originally came to see me because her family was going through a tough time with Sarah's older brother. He had been experimenting with drugs and alcohol. His experimentation evolved into abusing both substances on a regular basis. He had gotten himself into quite a bit of trouble, and therefore Sarah's family was spending an enormous amount of time, energy and money to help him.

Unfortunately, during this difficult time in Sarah's family, she felt invisible. She loved her brother very much but really wanted her parents also to pay attention to her and her needs. Naturally, Sarah started looking for new things to do, hoping that her parents would take notice. During eighth grade, Sarah decided she wanted to be more religious but didn't find her family's church very appealing. She began looking into other religions to find a faith that would be meaningful to her.

Sarah had two older cousins whom she was close to and admired. They were experimenting with the Wiccan faith. From my limited knowledge of Wicca, I could see why Sarah and her cousins found it interesting. They enjoyed the mysterious aspect of conducting spells, lighting candles and preserving nature—all things a curious eighth-grader would find appealing. Sarah's experiment worked in that she found something interesting to occupy her curiosities, and this religion was different enough that she was able to get the attention of her parents. In fact, her parents were panicked that Sarah wanted to become a "witch" and were desperate not to lose her to something they didn't understand, as they had with her brother.

I encouraged Sarah's mother to see her daughter's newfound interest for exactly what it was, experimentation and a cry for attention. I explained that Sarah was just trying on something new to see how it fit. I suggested that the mother join Sarah in going to the Wiccan church and participating with her. That way she could keep an eye on Sarah, as well as providing what her daughter really wanted, attention from her parents. It would also give Sarah's mom an opportunity to help Sarah put her exploration into context with their family values.

Did Sarah become a religious fanatic, or harm herself or anyone else during the process? No. If anything, this provided an opportunity for Sarah's family to accept something that was important to her. It was a way for them to show an interest in something positive she was doing rather than spending all their energy on the negative behaviors of her brother.

The reason for sharing this example is to illustrate that experimenting isn't always bad. In fact, it is a very good and necessary part of growing up. The key is to handle your children's experimentation with a calm resolve and understanding. That isn't to say that you can't be firm or insist they avoid things that are illegal or dangerous, but a bit of compassion for trying something new can often ward off more serious experimentation.

Often, your children's ideas come from how they think you may or may not react to their behavior. When your child comes home with purple spiked hair, the best thing you can do is say, "Interesting new hairdo. Maybe it will go with your tie-dyed T-shirt." This type of reaction lets your child know that you noticed what he or she has done and accept him or her, no matter what the hair color. It also lets your child know that you understand how hard it is to be an adolescent and that trying a new hair color is all part of that process.

Also, don't underestimate the power of peer pressure. If your child experiments with something that isn't considered "in" or "cool" with their peers, it probably won't last long. So don't get too worked up about the small things. Natural consequences such as going to school with purple spiked hair and having all your friends laugh at you won't be fun for your child but will have a greater impact on his or her future behavior than your grounding him or her for life because of looking ridiculous.

Sex, drugs and rock 'n' roll

Traditionally, this is what has scared parents most—their kids getting involved with sex, drugs and rock 'n' roll. The specifics vary by generation, but any combination of these activities brings some grief to most parents.

Also, sex, drugs and rock 'n' roll tend to be topics talked about widely in society and in the media. In many cases, these issues tend to center on high school-age children, but the reality is that these interests begin earlier. Society doesn't always want to admit it, but these issues are prevalent in our middle schools, so as parents, you need to be aware and informed.

Let's start with drugs. A wide variety of drugs are obtainable anywhere in the United States, including middle schools. This is an issue that spans all cities, communities and neighborhoods. There is no discrimination based on education or economic status. Access to drugs is quite easy, if you are looking. This is not to scare you but to help you understand the issue and help your kids avoid it.

The good news is that the majority of middle-school students don't seek out drugs or people who use them, but some do. And that brings us to a bigger question: why. Why do some students get mixed up with the wrong crowd and/or with drugs?

During middle school, students are desperately looking for their identity as young adults. They feel "in between," as they are not children anymore but they aren't grown up either. Their bodies and minds are hard-wired to search for who they are and what they want to become. As part of this search, there is a natural insecure feeling as everything in their world is changing. Some children make it through this transition more easily than others. It is the children who struggle through this transition that are most at risk for drugs and other self-destructive behavior.

There is no magic formula to keep kids from using drugs, but there are things to watch out for while they are going through this life transformation and proactive things you can do to help your child make smart choices about drugs and other possibly harmful temptations.

First, it is important to keep in mind that not everyone who tries a cigarette or marijuana becomes a drug abuser or advances to trying more serious drugs. Kids are naturally curious, and some satisfy their natural curiosity by trying something once and even a handful of times and then move on with their lives in another direction. But some are more than curious and are looking to fill a void; maybe they are looking for companionship, acceptance or approval, for example. These kids may feel disenfranchised with peers and find comfort with the drug culture and a sense of community that comes with joining a group of kids using drugs. Let's explore this idea a bit further.

Throughout our lives, we all tend to gather with people similar to ourselves or join a group in which we have something in common with the members. Middle- school students are no different. A middle school is a community with various groups, and all kids want to find their place in this community whether they are actually able to communicate this need or not.

Any middle-school student would be able to identify these groups within this community for you easily. She can tell you who the kids in the popular group are, who the jocks are, who the computer geeks are, who the skaters and gamers are. She can also tell you the characteristics of the members who make up each group. For instance, what they wear, where they eat lunch on campus, where they hang out after school, what type of music they like.

And because middle school is a time in these children's lives when they are growing, changing and finding themselves, they don't all fit into one of the established groups at school. They may feel like outsiders and as a way of rebelling against the naturally created established groups (i.e. cliques), they form their own group. The unaffiliated come together to affiliate on their own terms and in their own way. A student once described them as the "unpopular but don't care" clique. Students in these groups are often very accepting of others who feel different and/or left out of the more traditional cliques at school.

Yet being in one of these "unpopular, but don't care" groups often makes them at risk for self-destructive behavior. These groups tend to be rebellious in nature. They tend to hang out in more secluded areas of the campus, do poorly in school even if they are very bright, and they may have low self-esteem. Put it all together and you have a recipe for dangerous behavior. And unfortunately, drugs can be a way for students like these to escape and numb the difficult feelings that they are experiencing. A very dangerous combination.

There is another high-risk group of kids that is much more difficult to identify. Research has shown that some people (including kids) have body chemistry that makes them more susceptible to addiction. This can be any type of addiction—alcohol, drugs, food, gambling, even exercise. This chemical imbalance can cause people to constantly try to repeat or improve upon the short-term euphoric feeling that comes from using an addictive substance. This effort then fuels their addiction and associated behavior. Unfortunately, this chemical imbalance can be very disruptive to a growing child and should be reviewed by a physician as soon as this type of problem is suspected. If you suspect your child may have this type of tendency, please talk to your pediatrician and explore it further.

Prevention

As a parent, the best thing you can do to prevent your children from abusing drugs is to "be aware" and "be there." Your involvement in their lives, friendships and activities is the most important way to help prevent this type of dangerous behavior. Know who your children hang out with at school, meet their friends and their friends' parents, spend time with your children doing things they enjoy (even if you don't), and keep your children involved in extracurricular activities that give them positive experiences and role models. Speak to your children openly, and fully listen to them often. Children involved in drugs probably won't come out and tell you directly, but you will start seeing changes in their behavior that will be concerning. Listen to your gut. If you suspect that your child is involved with drugs, don't be afraid of embarrassing or upsetting him. Be watchful and talk to his friends' parents about your concerns. Come together with the other parents as a community to help all of the kids. None of these steps are easy, but they are completely necessary to keep your child safe and healthy.

Getting help

If you feel that your child is doing drugs, seek help immediately. Many parents feel ashamed or embarrassed about asking for this type of help, but it is the only way. It isn't your fault that your child is in trouble, but not acting would be.

Start by contacting your pediatrician for a referral to a teen drug specialist in your community. Also, your school's administrators can be a good resource. They can help you get access to a school nurse and/or school counselor trained specifically to help children with this issue. Another option is to contact your local police department as it also may have dedicated resources (resource officers, programs, community outreach) specifically to work with young people who have drug issues.

All of these professionals are trained to provide you confidential help, knowing that this information is sensitive. These are people you can trust to handle your family's situation appropriately. Drug use is a serious situation in which your child needs your help, so stay strong and get the assistance your family needs.

One community of parents I met had decided to create a watchdog group of parents to help fight drugs among their kids.

Each parent signed an agreement to be watchful of certain signs and behaviors among their kids as well as their friends. The parents also agreed to contact one another if they noticed anything suspicious among the kids. I like this approach in that the parents pulled together to help keep the children of their community safe and healthy. I would only caution any parents interested in starting such a group to make sure you clearly express to your children the dangers of drugs and why you feel it is so important that they don't take part in these activities. It is really important to keep the lines of communication open with your own child as well as helping the community. You don't want your children to think that you and other parents will be sneaking around watching them. Educate your children and make sure you have their trust so that if they need help, they know they can come to you first.

At first, these efforts may upset your child but as a parent, you have to do what is right for him or her. Your child will thank you in the long run.

Experimenting with sex

During the middle-school years, our children begin experiencing the changes to enter adulthood—physically and emotionally. Each child enters puberty at a different rate, but most kids start seeing and feeling these changes during middle school. Puberty causes children to feel awkward, as if they no longer fit in their own skin. So, it's only natural to begin experimenting with their new skin to figure out how it fits.

Girls tend to begin these changes at a younger age than boys. You will often see girls at a middle school towering over boys of their same age. Girls tend to become intrigued with boys before boys even notice them. This can be an awkward dance of girls trying to grab attention from boys who are flattered that they have been chosen but really don't share the same interest yet. This is a time when boys and girls are both privately questioning their own sexuality and how their bodies are changing. It can be very confusing.

So they begin experimenting as a way of trying to make sense out of this confusion. This is also a time when kids give a great deal of importance to what their friends think and feel. This just exacerbates the confusion because all the kids are unsure about these feelings yet want to give the impression that they have it all figured out.

As adults, we know that sexual relationships are complex and confusing at any age, so we can understand how confusing it must be to have these feelings and changes happening while in middle school.

An eighth-grade girl came to me once explaining that she had a problem relating to boys. She claimed that when she interacted with boys, they got the wrong idea about her. She thought that she would use a certain "look" when talking with friends but that "look" would lead them to believe she was flirting with them. Boys would get the wrong idea and ask her to meet after school behind the gym to "make out." When she declined these offers, the boys became upset with her and accused her of leading them on and teasing them with her "look."

After some time, this girl felt she was developing a reputation for teasing boys and that they didn't want to be friends with her any longer. Unfortunately, these situations made her very self-conscience about the way she interacted with friends— boys and girls. She became worried about how she talked with friends and felt self-conscious about meeting new people and trying to make new friends.

This is a perfect example of how young these middle-school students really are and how their experimenting in the areas of relationships can be very difficult. Relationships are mostly about communication, and at this stage of development children's ability to communicate with one another is limited, making relationships tricky at best.

A first crush

Crushes seem to be the most common type of relationship that middle-school students venture into. Crushes often escalate into a "going out" relationship in which they don't actually go anywhere but rather declare their "like" for one another. These relationships are often short-lived. They can be as short as a 45-minute sixth-period science class or as long as a week.

Crushes tend to stir quite a bit of drama and emotion with the kids who are participating as well as their group of friends. Middle-school students, girls especially, don't do anything alone. So any relationship or news that affects one friend often affects the whole group.

These relationships tend to be sweet and harmless and are all part of the experimentation that goes along with growing up. But there are a few trends with middle-school relationships that should concern parents. One is the aggressive nature that some girls have adopted when it comes to boys. Since girls tend to become interested in boys at a younger age, they often are the ones to initiate the connection.

For example, one girl will mention to a friend that she thinks a boy in her math class is cute. That friend is sworn to secrecy of this sensitive information but then passes a note about it to another friend at lunch. By the end of the school day, the chosen boy is being teased about his new girlfriend, and the girl with the crush is chasing him around the playground. And the boy isn't sure exactly what has transpired and how he got involved.

In some cases, girls are even more forward in initiating a relationship with a boy. Girls will call a boy's home constantly, spend hours e-mailing him, stop by his home or follow his every move around the school campus. The amount of aggression that girls are willing to show is quite concerning. A girl often will become obsessed with her efforts to catch a boy's attention while she enjoys being the ringleader of her circle of friends, who are going along for the ride.

I find this trend quite concerning, as some girls are willing to give up anything to get the attention of a certain boy. They give up their time, personal interests, self-esteem and good judgment while often putting themselves in unsafe situations to achieve their goal.

As parents, the best thing we can do to keep our children out of these situations is to help them develop a strong respect for themselves and their bodies. This is a life skill that they will carry with them now and into all of their future relationships. These skills are not built overnight but rather in an ongoing process that starts with setting a good example for our children. As a parent, make sure you're making good choices that are self-respecting in your own life, and talk to your children about those choices.

For example, a parent recently shared with me that her boss was treating her disrespectfully at work. He was making sarcastic remarks in front of others, teasing her, etc. At first, this parent was offended and embarrassed by her boss' actions but wasn't sure how to handle it. So she only complained at home, which her 12-year-old daughter heard loud and clear. Finally, her daughter said to her mom, "Why don't you just quit your job?" The mother then realized how much of an impression her relationships at work were having on her daughter. She explained to her daughter that quitting wasn't the answer. She liked her job and was successful at it but needed to stand up for herself and tell her boss that his comments were not acceptable.

Some of these life situations may be a bit complicated for our children to fully understand, but the important lessons can be broken down and either explained or modeled so that our children can then have the personal strength to handle difficult situations in their lives.

Another trend that parents should be aware of is that when children begin experimenting with sexual activities, they realize the risks of sexual intercourse and will experiment with an "everything but intercourse" approach. This can include anything from kissing to oral sex and can be just as confusing and emotionally dangerous for children as having intercourse. The feelings associated with sharing your body in this way are complex. Boys and girls have different emotions and sexual drives, making this type of behavior even more complex and confusing.

There is also an interesting myth that tends to travel around middle-school circles with girls. They think that having sexual intercourse changes them in some way so that once they have been sexually active, there is no turning back and they will then always be sexually active. The problem with this line of thinking is that if a girl does have sexual intercourse but then decides it was the wrong decision, she feels that she is scarred or marked for life by that decision. It is important for children to know that there are life-changing consequences to becoming sexual active but if they have made a mistake, they can choose a different path and not continue that type of activity.

There are a number of good organizations trying to help give kids the education to make good decisions about their own bodies and behavior. Find one in your community that fits within your family values and share this information with your child. Educating children about how to handle themselves in a difficult situation is the best thing you can do to help keep them safe and healthy.

Music

Whatever music is popular among your children and their friends, there is no conclusive evidence to show it has an effect on their decision-making or judgment. Music of all kinds is an art form, and we should encourage our children to enjoy it.

But again, it is most important for you to know what type of music your children are listening to, even if you hate it. Familiarize yourself with the artists they enjoy and the social movement surrounding this type of music. By doing this, you are showing your children how much their interests matter to you while having the opportunity to put the type of music they enjoy into context with the values and behaviors that are important to you and your family.

Additionally, the type of music a child is listening to may be very telling of whom he is hanging out with, what group he is associating with and what type of behaviors he may be considering. Again, I don't believe that musical lyrics make kids do certain things, but I do know that listening to certain types of music will help your child associate with certain groups of kids and as a parent, it is important for you to know as much as possible about who is listening to what.

In my high school, there was a clique known as the "Rockers." And yes, they were known for listening to rock music. But they were also known for hanging out in the parking lot, smoking cigarettes and skipping school. Did rock music make them do those things? Of course not. But if you were considered a "Rocker" or wanted to be in with the "Rockers," then you conformed.

Listen to your gut

How can you help your children make good choices about their behavior? Teach them to trust their own judgment and listen to their gut feelings. Whenever any of us are in a difficult situation, we get a gut feeling. You either have a good feeling or a bad feeling based on the situation. This type of gut feeling comes naturally, so our job as parents is to help our children learn to listen to these feelings and act accordingly. Don't ignore them and then make a bad decision.

Whenever I am working with a child who has broken a rule or done something wrong, I always ask whether he/she knew it was wrong when the situation occurred. I ask whether the child got a feeling way down in his or her stomach that this was a very bad idea. These children always say "yes, but I did it anyway." The good news is that they got the feeling. The bad news is that they didn't listen to it. I always tell children, "You have good judgment; you just have to listen to it and act accordingly."

Learning how to use your gut feeling is an amazing way to give children power when faced with making hard choices. This skill may be the key to helping your child experiment while staying safe and out of trouble.

Again, the best thing parents can do is to "be aware" and "be there" for your children during this time, as well as helping them develop some life skills around using their own judgment when in a difficult or confusing situation.

Chapter 8

Navigating the school system

Like any organization or business, middle schools are run by a system. It will make your life a lot easier if you learn this system and how to work within it for the three years that your child will be attending a middle school. The system at your school may vary slightly from the information I give you here, but the point is to learn whatever system it uses. Learning the system will help you be more connected to what your child is experiencing as well as give you a leg up when your child may try to test the limits on how much more he or she knows about the system than you do. For instance, if your son or daughter comes home and says there is no homework that night, you should know two things about the middle school system. One is that there is hardly ever a night in middle school when your child truly has no homework. Math teachers are the most notorious for never letting a day go by without a homework assignment. And on the rare occasion that a math teacher goes easy for one night, there is always a long-term project to work on or an upcoming test to study for. Secondly, most middle schools have some sort of system in which parents and students can find out what homework has been assigned. There is typically a homework hotline or a homework Website on which you and your child can make sure that there is no homework for a given evening.

As you probably already know, schools are not known for their communication skills. They will often send a lot of information home to parents in different formats and different media. This can be really confusing in elementary school, but it gets exponentially worse in middle school. Again, do what you can to figure out what communication tools are being used and the timing of these communications. In the beginning, make sure to read everything carefully. It is really important to go to the meetings held at the beginning of the school year or even during the summer before school begins. Most schools do some sort of registration or open-house event for new incoming students. Do your best to attend. Very valuable information will be given at these events, and schools may be reluctant to help parents who don't attend. If you aren't able to attend in person, send a family member or good family friend to represent you and gather the information on your behalf.

Do yourself a favor and become very familiar with the school's Website. Use this as your first resource when looking for answers, forms, documents, calendars and other information. Schools spend an enormous amount of time and energy making their Websites full of information so that they won't have to answer the same questions over and over. If you call the school with an inquiry, the staff is likely to send you to the Website. So save yourself some time and start there. If you can't find what you are looking for, then contact either the teacher or school office. If you aren't computer-savvy, your child probably can help you access the information. If you don't have access to the Internet from your home or office, the public library is always a good option. Or you might try asking the school if there is a computer that could be used in the school library, office or computer lab. Some schools have work space set aside for volunteers, and there may be a computer with Internet access there.

The big message here is to stay on top of the paper work and the many dates/deadlines. Middle schools have many families and students to take care of, so they send out a lot of information and leave it up to the parents to filter and assimilate it. It isn't easy at first, but soon you will find some order to this system. For example, maybe a monthly newsletter is sent to your home the first week of every month. I have found that many parents get overwhelmed by the amount of information being thrown at them when their children enter middle school. So develop your own system to manage this information flow in the beginning to make sure you don't miss anything important. Once you and your child get in the middle-school groove, you will know which pieces of information are really important and what you can ignore.

School staff

One of the best places to learn how a middle school works is by getting to know the staff in the main office. These people can be your gateway to, or gatekeepers of, almost everything you will need at the school. I suggest getting to know the people who work in the office and make sure they like you. Most office staff members really appreciate a plate of cookies or a note to the principal saying what a good job they have done. Small gestures like these create an enormous amount of goodwill, which you will need at some point while your child attends that school. I have found most people who work in the main office at a school are caring and helpful. But middle schools are very busy places, and the office staff gets asked to do a lot for a lot of people. Having some sort of personal connection with them will help when you need something for your child in one of those really hectic times.

Most middle schools have at least a small staff of administrators as well as some additional resource staff who may be helpful to you, so it is a good idea to find out who is there and what they do. Often middle schools will have a school principal and a vice principal, but when the district is looking for ways to cut back, the position of vice principal is sometimes eliminated. The principal's role in a school is vast. That person is responsible for everything that happens on the campus, including the performance of the staff, the students and the facility itself. It is a very large job, and the principals whom I have met are very good at what they do. If your child's school is fortunate enough to have a vice principal as well, the principal and vice principal often divide certain responsibilities for the staff and students to help manage the large amount of work. As you get to know them, it will be helpful to find out how they divide the responsibilities. I probably wouldn't worry about this right away because if you have an issue that you feel the principal or vice principal should know about, don't hesitate to call either of them and he or she will refer you to the right person if necessary.

If you have an issue with your child in middle school, I would first recommend contacting the teacher or teachers who may have some insights into the issue. As in any system, there is a hierarchy in schools, and the best place to begin is with the classroom teacher. If you don't get satisfaction with the teacher, then I recommend escalating your concern to the principal or vice principal. Never be afraid to expose a classroom issue to the administrators, as I am sure they do their best to stay on top of any problems on their campus, but there may be things going on in a classroom that they aren't aware of and that would interest them highly.

There are also a number of other staff members at a middle school who offer resources that may be helpful for your family. Most middle schools have at least a part-time school counselor. In some schools this person may be called a guidance counselor. A school or guidance counselor can be a good resource on a number of topics such as why your child is taking a certain combination of classes or what other classes may be available or appropriate for your child. A counselor can offer advice on how to handle peer relationships with which you or your child may be struggling. They can also be a referral source for a number of community services such as counseling, tutoring, doctors, parent education, after-school programs, summer programs and much more.

Middle school will also have a school nurse, but this person may be assigned to a number of schools so will physically be at your school only part-time. If you have a health or nutrition question, ask the office staff how you can contact the school nurse. They will most likely have a schedule of the days he or she will be at your child's school as well as a pager or phone number where the nurse can be reached. Each state has different standards for health screenings that are conducted in middle school, and the nurse can tell you what your child will be tested for and why. Most school districts require written notification of these screenings beforehand, so watch for those as well.

Other staff positions will vary a lot from school to school or within your school district, but the main point here is to get to know what resources your school offers. School districts offer lots of services to the families they serve, but they don't always do a good job of advertising these resources.

Communicating with teachers

I wish I could give you an easy formula for communicating with your child's middle-school teachers, but the fact is that your child will have five or six teachers a day, and each of them may have a different preferred way of communicating with the parents.

This is one of my biggest pet peeves with school districts. I believe that they should ask all the teachers to communicate with parents in a similar way. For example, all teachers would be expected to read their e-mail daily and respond to parents within 24 hours. Or all teachers would be required to listen to their mail messages at the end of the school day and respond to parents by the end of the following school day. From my experience, the districts and individual schools have few guidelines or requirements for teachers to follow when communicating with parents. This can be very frustrating for parents. For this reason, to communicate effectively with your child's middle school teachers, you are going to have to figure out how each one of them prefers to talk with you. At the beginning of the year, I would recommend simply asking them for the best way to reach them and what response time you can expect.

Schools offer teachers a number of communication tools such as voicemail, e-mail, Websites, paper messages taken by the staff in the main office, phones in the classroom, mailings that are either sent home or given to your child to bring home, and others. The problem is that each teacher picks a preferred method of communication, and some teachers let parents know their preferred methods and some don't. I had a mom call me one day so frustrated that her daughter's math teacher would not return her calls. She explained that she had left numerous messages on the teacher's voicemail. Of course, I knew exactly which math teacher she was referring to, as this particular teacher refused to use voicemail and would communicate with parents only via e-mail. I felt silly explaining this teacher's preference to this frustrated parent, as it just seemed ridiculous to me that she would refuse to use voicemail, yet that was the situation.

But with that said, let's put ourselves in a teacher's shoes for a minute. Most middle-school teachers see 180 students per day and each one of them may have two parents or step-parents and often other family members such as grandparents, aunts and uncles who are very interested in their progress at school. Teachers are afraid of getting overwhelmed by the volume of information that they need to give to families, so they pick a way to manage that information incoming and outgoing. I think we would all agree that teachers need a way to manage the needs of so many students and their families, but what I find frustrating is that there is no standardized process that parents can learn and follow. So it will be up to you as a parent to find out how your child's teachers will best communicate with you.

Students also must learn how to effectively communicate with teachers. Middle-school students are often hesitant to talk to teachers directly and therefore are commonly misunderstood by a teacher or get disciplinary action for behavior that may be easily avoided. Teachers each have their own styles and their own rules for the classroom. Teachers are also individuals and therefore all have different personalities and temperaments. I have found that any child can be successful in a class if he can learn what each teacher expects and identify their individual hot buttons. With a little coaching, children can learn to read a teacher's mood from the minute they walk into the classroom and therefore act accordingly. Helping students learn these important life skills has proven to be very useful. The main point is that kids and teachers can avoid a lot of the typical classroom management issues if children are able to read the situation.

For instance, let's say your child has a math teacher who is quite serious and businesslike. Yet your child is very social and likes to catch up with all of his/her friends upon entering the classroom. This math teacher typically gives one or two warnings before sending kids out of class for talking. Now if your child walks into class one day and notices that his/her math teacher has an irritated look on his face and wasn't at the door greeting the students as usual, that could be a clue to your child that today isn't a good day to talk with friends at the beginning of class. In fact if he/she does, this math teacher may not give any warnings today and may send people out of class right away.

Body language, facial expressions and tone of voice can tell us a lot about a person's mood, including a teacher's. Help your child read these non-verbal communication signs so he/she can better handle the situation the student is walking into each day. Another way you can help your child work with teachers is to identify and understand each of their "hot buttons." Every teacher (and person, for that matter) has certain things that bother him or her. I call these their "hot buttons." Learning what a teacher's hot buttons are can prevent a lot of hassles for a student and the teacher. Children are very perceptive. I'll bet if you ask your kids what a particular teacher's hot buttons are, they would be able to tell you. The trick is helping your kids understand this concept and showing them how avoiding these hot buttons will help them be more successful in class.

I wish I could tell you that all teachers are unbiased and never put labels on children, but I can't. So do what you can to make sure you child gets a fair reputation. Often when a teacher labels a student as a talker or as someone who fools around in class, that child will get punished unfairly or hastily. Teaching your children how to read the mood of the teacher and the classroom will help them avoid those problems.

Organization

Middle-school students have a lot to keep track of, as they have five or six classes a day. Each class has a different teacher, different class rules, different homework assignments. All of these details can be overwhelming for a new sixth-grader. These are big changes from elementary school.

Middle schools rely heavily on the "planner" system. Each student gets his or her own planner (or agenda, or organizer) at the beginning of the year. The planners include a calendar with all of the school holidays, a list of school rules and some fun pictures and trivia facts that appeal to kids this age. The planners are the heart of staying organized in middle school. All the teachers expect students to write their homework assignments in their planners each day. Parents are asked to sign the planners and are encouraged to use them as a way to send notes back and forth between parents and teachers. Students are asked to keep their planners neat and organized and always with them. It is always a lot of fun to see what the planners look like a week or so into the school year. Let's just say many of them would probably make a great exhibit in a modern art museum. Each gets uniquely decorated and personalized based on the creativity of its owner.

Some students use their planners very effectively. They may highlight certain school projects in a certain color to remind them of due dates or add stickers to the days on which they have tests. Each planner is an original work of art. Some planners would never leave the student's backpack unless a teacher or parent specifically asked to see it. These are typically the students who think that if they don't write a homework assignment into their planner, then it doesn't really exist.

Use the planner method to your advantage. It can be a great bridge of communication between you and your child's teachers. Make sure your child knows that the planner is a family resource, not a secret place for them to hide schoolwork.

Grades

I personally feel there is much too much emphasis put on what grades students get in middle school rather than assessing what they have actually learned. With that said, most parents want their children to do well, and the only tangible way to measure that in today's school system is through grades. I do remind parents often that when a child is applying for Harvard Medical School or working on a certificate to become a teacher, no one goes back and looks to see what grade they got in sixth-grade core class. I say this because grades don't always tell the whole story. They usually are an indication of something that we need to investigate and to identify the root of the real issue.

So let's start with the beginning. How do teachers develop grades? Most teachers will explain their formulas and criteria at the beginning of the school year. I realize there is a lot of information given to parents at the start of every school year, and this seems to be a piece that parents tend to ignore. I would suggest you give the grading structure a second look so that as the school year progresses you will understand where the teacher is placing the most emphasis.

In most cases, grades are determined on a point system. Teachers apply a certain point value to each test, quiz, homework assignment, long-term project or other work. They then grade your child's work and give it some number of points relative to the total points possible for that assignment. Unlike in elementary school, graded tests, quizzes and assignments taken in middle school never seem to make it home for you to see. To your child's credit, even if the work is good and scored high points, it may not make it home. Middle-school students have so much paper to keep track of and so much on their minds that papers tend not to make it home. Or if they do, they are hidden in the black hole your child calls a backpack.

Many parents seem to be shocked when their children's grades arrive, yet I have found that if the child's grades are good you don't hear much about it. If the child's grades are poor, someone at the school gets a phone call.

Most middle schools give some sort of update on students' progress every nine weeks throughout the school year. Often the first information sent home is a progress report. Some schools require the teachers to send home a progress report only if the student is struggling or in danger of failing the course. Others require a progress report to go home for every student. I prefer the latter, but you may want to check and see what the policy is at your child's school. Progress reports are just a way to inform parents. They do not go into your child's permanent school record. They can be a wake-up call. If your child gets a poor progress report, there is still half a semester to address the issue, so it is time to take some action. I recommend scheduling a meeting with your child and the teacher to see what can be done to help your child. Also remember that this system is far from perfect and mistakes can be made, such as a teacher's forgetting to enter a grade for a completed assignment, so if you feel your child has gotten an unfair comment or grade on a progress report, make sure to investigate.

Report cards usually come out at the end of the first semester and then at the end of the school year. These grades do go into your child's permanent education record, but again, let's keep them in perspective. Poor grades are a sign that something is wrong. It doesn't necessarily mean your child isn't smart or capable. I believe it is a parent's job to be involved in the child's education so that grades are never shocking and to provide the support the child needs to do well. The point of education is to learn, not to get a certain grade point average. If you feel strongly that your child has done the best he can in a difficult pre-algebra class and has learned a lot, then a "C" may be a perfectly acceptable grade.

Homework

The reality is that middle-school teachers give a lot of homework. Some courses tend to require more homework than others, but teachers have an enormous amount of curriculum that they need to teach and very little actual teaching time in the classroom. Therefore, teachers rely heavily on sending assignments and projects home to reinforce the concepts covered in class. Middle school is also a time when students need to begin learning the art of studying. Most students don't really understand that concept at first. They think if no homework assignment is given, they are free. This is not the case if your child is going to not only keep up but also excel in middle school.

Parents and students alike have complaints about homework. Some of these complaints are valid, and others may be coming from a student who would rather be playing video games or talking on the phone than doing anything related to school. This section of the book will address many of these issues, but homework is a fact of life in middle school. One of the teachers I worked with used to dress up every year for Halloween as "The Homework Witch." She was an exceptional core teacher who was able to make light of a daily fact that her students and their families dealt with. If it makes you feel any better, remember that every homework assignment a teacher gives to his or her class has to be graded and recorded, multiplied by the number of students in that teacher's five or six daily classes. That usually adds up to about 150 papers per assignment.

Why does there seem to be so much homework in middle school? Traditionally, the purpose of homework was to give students practice in a new concept learned that day in school. The brain needs time and repetition to master new skills, so the teacher begins that process in the classroom and then assigns homework that evening to reinforce that learning. Today, homework has taken a slightly expanded role in that process. Teachers are under an enormous amount of pressure due to factors such as state education standards, over-sized classrooms, students with various educational and emotional needs, and an ever-increasing reliance on test scores for budgeting. As a result, teachers have less actual instruction time during classes, so they rely more on homework assignments to cover the necessary curriculum. Teachers are being squeezed, so your child gets more homework. Is giving more homework the answer? Probably not, but it is the reality.

One thing that I think is important to remember when it comes to homework or any other issue your child may have at school: As parents, you are solely responsible for your children and their needs. You are their advocates and often their voice. So, please remember that you can and should question any practice a teacher may be using that you feel is inappropriate, including giving too much homework. I have seen many teachers and parents come to understand one another's position and be able to find a workable compromise on lots of issues, including homework. Also, if your child is having a lot of trouble doing her homework, it may be a sign of another problem. She may need glasses or testing for a learning disability. For example, I have experienced situations in which a student is spending an excessive amount of time trying to get through a few math problems that were assigned for homework. When the parents spoke to the teacher and explained how long it was taking their child to do each homework problem, it was clear to the teacher that the concept wasn't covered thoroughly enough in class that day, so he would re-teach the concept the next day.

My point is, don't hesitate to talk with a teacher about your concerns with your child's homework. He is probably not the only student experiencing this problem, and most teachers I have worked with are reasonable and willing to work through these issues.

On the other side of the homework issue, my favorite line from a middle-school student is that when a parent asks a seventh-grader if he has any homework to do tonight, he answers, "Oh no, I finished it at school." Yes, it is true that many teachers will give students a few minutes at the end of the class period to start a homework assignment, but I will guarantee you that there is rarely a night in middle school that your student doesn't have something to do for homework. Even if a student is able to rush through a homework assignment during the time at the end of class, there is always more to do. Middle school is when students begin doing projects, and there is always a need to study for an upcoming quiz or test. Studying will be covered later in this section.

If your child is not doing homework or not turning in completed assignments, here are a few tactics I would suggest implementing.

First, begin a backpack clean-out day. I would suggest picking a day in the middle of the week so that if completed assignments are found, they can still be turned in that week. The same reasoning goes for incomplete assignments. If you find out work hasn't been done by Wednesday, the teacher may still accept it if turned in by the end of that week. Losing a few points for turning in a late assignment is better than getting a zero for failing to return it. Students' backpacks tend to turn into the black hole of paper. I am not sure there is anything we can do to get middle-school students to keep their backpacks more organized, but a weekly clean-out really helps.

Second, be sure to review your child's planner daily. As mentioned previously, most middle schools use some sort of planner or organizer system to help students keep track of their assignments. From my experience, most students start out keeping their planners very neat and filled out in the beginning of sixth grade. Depending on the student, the organization and use of the planner begins to fall off quickly. By seventh grade, the planners are mostly used for scribbling, recording friends' birthdays and marking school holidays.

Planners not only are a tool for students but also can be used as a tool for parents as well. A daily review of your child's planner will reveal a lot. It will tell you whether your child has written down homework assignments. If not, you can then call a friend in the class or the homework hotline to find out whether an assignment was really given. Ask your child to note in the planner that no homework has been assigned for that night if that's the case. That way, you know that your son or daughter at least opened the planner and has written something down for class that day. I will offer you this: If homework is an issue in your house, I promise you that the day you stop checking the planner is the day your child stops using it.

You can also use the planners as a communication tool between you and the teachers. Most teachers have some sort of checking system for the planners whether it is daily or weekly. You can write a note to the teacher in your child's planner and ask for a signature or a response. This is a quick way for you and the teacher to share information, and it is your child's responsibility to make it happen. This system works well for some students, and for others it won't work at all. If you are getting a lot of excuses as to why the teacher hasn't signed your child's planner or hasn't written back to you, call the teacher directly.

Third, get a large wall calendar at home where you can write in long-term assignments as well as quizzes and shorter-term work. That way, when your child says she has no homework or that she has finished everything, you can use the calendar to remind her of what is coming up.

And last, if homework has become a major issue for you and your child, I would suggest the following method along with the suggestions given above. Most schools have some sort of weekly progress report system. Under this system, the student picks up a form in the office once a week, usually on a certain day. It is the student's responsibility to take this form to each of his/her teachers that day and get a report of how they have done that week. This can be for homework assignments, behavior or both. Then the form is brought home for a parent's signature. If you are going to use this system, I recommend having a reward/consequence system attached to it. In other words, if the progress report comes back satisfactory, your child gets a reward. If it does not come back satisfactory, there is some sort of disciplinary action attached. The trick to making this system work is the following. First, you have to set specific parameters as to what is satisfactory and what is not satisfactory on the progress report. Be specific because your child will be looking for loopholes in the system. Second, let your child pick the reward and or the disciplinary action ahead of time. Again, give them parameters to stay within, but I have found that students are much more likely to work for something that they have picked. On the other side of that, they are often harder on themselves than we would be with a punishment, but they can't argue about the discipline they prescribed for themselves.

Most importantly, don't let homework get in the way of your relationship with your child. I understand how frustrating it can be when your child isn't doing schoolwork to the standard you know he or she is capable of. But try to remember that homework in middle school is not necessarily an indicator of success in adult life. Homework must be done for a student to succeed in school, but it doesn't have to be the cause of World War III in your home. Follow the suggestions above calmly, without anger. Just make it part of your home routine and spend your energy on more enjoyable things with your child. You will both get more out of it.

Projects

Part of the curriculum for middle school is to learn how to do long- and short-term projects. Short-term projects could be due within one or two days or perhaps a week after the assignment is given. A long-term project often has multiple components, possibly some group work, and a due date that may be three to four weeks or longer after the assignment is given. With long-term projects most teachers give deadlines along the way. For instance, they may ask the students to turn in a first draft or one component of the project before the final project is due. The idea here is to teach students time management, a big theme in the middle-school curriculum.

Keeping track of these projects and all the pieces that go with them isn't easy for you or your child. This is where the large wall calendar comes in handy. I suggest putting the project deadlines on the calendar and then helping your son or daughter break the project down into smaller pieces, setting your own deadlines for each of these. That will help your child not to feel overwhelmed by a large project and will help him/her stay on track to finish before the final due date. Some teachers will break the project into components with their own deadlines for your student, but if they don't, it is important to help your child do this.

Group projects are another aspect of the middle-school curriculum. Your child's reaction to being assigned a group project may tell you a lot about what type of student he or she is. If your child comes home complaining about the group that he has been assigned to work with, saying he just knows he will get stuck with all the work, you know you have a hard-working, studious child. If she is thrilled that this is a group project rather than an individual one, you might be concerned that your child is looking for an easy way out of working hard.

Either way, you can have a role in helping your child learn how to find a happy medium while doing a group project. A group project is intended to teach your child the material at hand as well as how to work within a group that he may or may not like. As we all know, there are many times in life that we are forced to accomplish something with people we may not like. Group projects offer a way of introducing that life skill.

Again, I would recommend plotting out the due dates and milestones of a group project on the hanging wall calendar at home. You also may want to help by letting the group meet at your home at a time when you will be there to supervise. Teachers usually give groups time to meet at school, but if that isn't enough, you could help your child set up a conference call on the phone or a time to meet after school in the library. I stress the supervision part of these plans, as most middle-school students don't have the self-discipline to work effectively in a group without some supervision.

At times middle-school students get very excited about projects and come up with grand plans for what they want to create, such as extravagant videos or life-size statues. It may be up to you to give a reality check as to what is possible with the time and resources allotted for the project. If you feel the expectations of a project seem extreme, you may want to get clarification from the teacher as to what was actually assigned. Students can get carried away with their enthusiasm for a project, and you shouldn't feel that parents are expected to spend a lot of time or money on it. The purpose is for the students to use their creativity and time, not yours.

Again, a perfect time to work on projects is when your son or daughter comes home and tells you he/she finished all his/her homework at school earlier that day. Take a look at the wall calendar and see what is coming up.

Studying and taking tests

When homework really is done and there are no projects coming up, students often think they are in the clear. But actually this is a perfect time to do some studying. I personally believe that our school system isn't doing a very good job of teaching our kids how to study. Studying is an invaluable skill for college, not to mention how useful it is in our adult lives. Some schools offer a class in study skills at the beginning of middle school. I would recommend asking your child's middle school whether it offers a class like this. This is a great way to get started on learning the art of studying. If your school doesn't offer such a class, I recommend you do your best to help your child with this.

The large calendar mapping out projects, quizzes and tests is your first tool to helping your child study. See what is coming up and what he/she could begin preparing for in advance. Once you have identified what needs to be studied, the best way to learn something is to repeat it and then be able to explain it or show someone else how to do it.

Given that, if your child is trying to learn some reading material, have him or her read it through the first time. Then, he/she should read it again and highlight major points. Then have your child tell you about what he read. Next ask him to write down the main points in a notebook. Last, ask him to tell you what this reading material is about. If your child takes these steps, he will have this material well learned and most likely will do well when tested on it.

I also recommend you help your child learn some basic test-taking strategies. For instance, when taking a test with multiple-choice answers, first eliminate the answers you know are not possible and then narrow the remaining choices. This will help your child pick the right multiple-choice answer by a simple process of elimination.

Some students suffer from test-taking anxiety. Many times the student knows the material being asked on the test but gets so nervous when looking at the test that she freezes and can't remember the answers. When I work with a student who has test-taking anxiety, I recommend adhering to the following process, step by step. Teach this process to your children and they are sure to be more relaxed and therefore will do better on their tests.

Step 1 – Eat breakfast on the day of the test.
Step 2 – Take a brief walk on the way to the test. During the walk, eat a small candy bar such as a Snickers (chocolate for energy/peanuts for brain power) and don't look at your notes for the test.

Step 3 – When you begin the test, go through and answer the easy questions first.

Step 4 – When you get to a question that you know the answer to but just can't remember it, sit back in your seat and do the following visualization:

Close your eyes and watch yourself washing your parent's car. Notice the details of what is around you such as what you are wearing, the weather, etc. While you're washing the car, all of a sudden water stops coming out of the hose. See yourself trying to figure out why the water stopped. Then notice that the hose is stuck under one of the car's tires, choking off the flow. Watch yourself bend down and move the hose from under the tire. Then watch the water flow again. Open your eyes, and you will remember the answer to the question.

How to study

There are a few key ways to create a good homework/study environment. First, there is the place. Many families set their children up with a nice desk in their room to do their work. But doing homework and studying can feel lonely and isolating to a child. Even though most of the work requires doing it alone, there is no reason the child has to be closed up in a room alone to work. So why not pick a place where your child can get work done but not necessarily be alone. I think the kitchen table is an ideal place to do homework. Basically, you need a place where there is room to spread out papers, has good lighting and is quiet but where your child will not necessarily be alone.

I also recommend setting aside a certain time of day for studying and homework. During this time, turn off the TV and let the answering machine or voicemail pick up calls.

If possible, set up a time for homework when one parent is home to offer guidance and help. Right before dinner seems to be a good time for homework/studying. That way your child has had some relaxation time after school and can focus on schoolwork again. If necessary, homework can be finished after dinner, with dinnertime being a good break from the books.

Total quiet isn't always the best way for people to concentrate. Your child may do better with some soft music playing in the background or the natural noise of dinner being put together in the kitchen while he is working. I worked with a family whose son was able to retain information best if he was moving. They used to take long walks in their neighborhood while discussing the information he needed to know for an upcoming test. Every child learns differently. Helping your child figure out how he/she learns best and then creating an appropriate learning environment will ensure success in school.

The bottom line is that homework isn't always fun, but it is generally necessary. Being involved in the details of your child's schoolwork sends a strong message that this work is important—just as your own work is important. If you don't get involved with your child's schoolwork, he may get the impression that it isn't important to you so why should it be important to him.

Physical education

Physical education is a requirement for all middle-school students, and I find that many students either love or hate this course. Students who are athletic and like sports obviously do well in PE. Students who have interests in areas other than sports may dislike PE class and therefore not do well. Either way, I find that there is a lot of exposure in PE classes in middle school, and feel parents should be aware of the dynamics their children face daily.

First of all, middle-school students are required to change their clothes for PE. Locker rooms are interesting places, and it may be in your best interest to help your child prepare for this environment. In some middle schools, the locker room is the only place where students are assigned actual lockers. Because of budget cuts and security issues, many middle schools have removed lockers from their campuses except for the gym locker rooms. There seems to be a fascination with being able to hide something in middle school, so having lockers can breed problems such as people putting things in other people's lockers or students leaving dirty clothes in lockers for weeks at a time. You will also hear of the occasional prank of students' trying to stuff another student into a locker. One issue with the locker rooms is that there are lots of students in there at the same time with little or no supervision. PE teachers are rushing to get equipment ready for class and are often talking to students one-on-one while the locker room is filled with students changing. Middle-school students need supervision at all times, and the locker room is no exception. If your school is asking for parent volunteers, I highly recommend you offer to help out with the PE classes, as they really need it.

Another issue with PE is that the classes are very large and often filled with students in various grades. Even if your child's PE class includes only students from his or her grade, there may be other classes on the field or in the gym at the same time. This can cause a number of problems. At times, older students will tease or bully younger students. Middle-school students are self-conscious enough without having older students to make them feel worse. Schools have large grass fields, and there may be areas beyond a teacher's view. This is an ideal scenario for a middle-school student who is looking for some trouble. If you are getting notices from your child's teacher saying that he/she isn't participating during PE class, please look into it carefully. I don't mean to be paranoid or make you feel that way, but the fact is that PE classes are not always the safest environments for our kids.

Lastly, the nature of PE is obviously physical. Middle-school students' developmental stage often turns this physical activity into an issue. Students don't have great impulse control at this age, and their bodies are awkward. They also haven't learned to control their emotions, and they can get angry and frustrated easily. This combination can make PE class not as safe as most parents would like. Again, offering to volunteer your time to help the PE teachers manage kids during this time of day is a good idea. If your child is having an issue, don't hesitate to go to the PE teacher directly and then to the administrators if you aren't satisfied.

Physical education class can be a lot of fun, and it is wonderful for the kids to use some physical energy rather than just sit at a desk all day. But I believe it is a class where our children aren't supervised adequately, given the nature of the course work. As an active parent, be aware of the situation your child is in during PE class. If you don't like what you see or hear, speak up until it gets fixed.

The best thing you can do is to lead your family in a healthy, physically active lifestyle. That way, your child will be physically fit for the requirements of PE even if he or she doesn't love all the activities during the class. If your child doesn't enjoy a certain sport that is part of the PE curriculum, encourage him to do the best he can and to remember that the class will move on to the next activity soon. The PE curriculum is created with variety in mind in the hopes of each student's finding something to enjoy so that fitness becomes a continuing part of life. But no matter what, your child should always be safe at school during any activity, including PE.

Making changes

During middle school, there will be a time when your child wants to change a class or even change schools. Difficult issues come up during middle school, and kids don't have the skills to handle these situations yet. It will be up you to decide whether the situation your child is struggling with is worthy of sticking it out to learn a life lesson or if it calls for a change. Changing classes is the most common request. There are times when a student and a certain teacher just don't get along or when a certain classmate impedes your child's ability to learn. These are difficult decisions. I will warn you that most schools don't like to switch students into different classes. Administrators are afraid that if they make such a change for one student, then many will make the same request. But that shouldn't matter to you. If you truly feel it is in the best interest of your child's education to change classes or schools, then fight for it.

When there appears to be a misunderstanding or a personality clash with a teacher, I recommend that you and your child meet with the teacher. Middle- school students tend to complain and be dramatic, so a meeting with the teacher will help you see whether your child is looking for an easy way out or if there is really a bad match. All kids learn differently, and by the time your child gets to middle school, you will have a good idea of what his or her dominant learning style is. Providing your child's teacher with some suggestions of how your child learns best may address the problem. The teacher may be willing to try focusing on your child's needs. Sometimes kids are fearful of teachers, but when they sit down and talk with them in a small meeting, they get to see them as real people and then feel more comfortable in their classes. Give this approach a try, and don't be afraid to ask for what you think is best for your child.

Changing schools works a bit differently. If your child has had disciplinary problems, then his or her school may welcome the opportunity for a transfer to another campus. I hate to say this, but it is true. Quite frankly, sometimes the best thing you can do is give your child a chance at a fresh start. If you feel he or she has gotten an unfair reputation or has gotten in with the wrong crowd, changing schools can be helpful. This is a big adjustment for kids, however, so I wouldn't make the decision lightly.

My favorite story about changing schools is about a sixth-grade girl named Valerie. She soon became known in our office as "Amnesia Girl."

Amnesia Girl

Valerie was 11 years old and in the 6th grade. She had brown hair, a very mature hair style yet a youthful face and body. Valerie was extremely bright, very articulate with an advance vocabulary for her age. At first glance, Valerie appears quite prim and proper yet isn't shy about expressing her opinions on a variety of topics and is very willing to strongly fight for a particular cause she feels strongly about.

One day I get a call from the PE teacher saying that Valerie was acting strangely in the locker room and asking could she please send her to my office. She explained that Valerie was withdrawn and unresponsive to questions and seemed off balance when walking. The PE teacher escorted Valerie to my office. I said hello to Valerie in a familiar way, as we knew each other well from our weekly Girl Talk club. Valerie had a blank look on her face and asked, "Who are you?" I responded, "Valerie, it is me, Ellen. You know, the school counselor from Girl Talk club." She responded, "What is Girl Talk?" That is when I knew something strange was going on.

Many thoughts went through my mind: Is this for real? Did she hit her head or injure herself somehow? Or is she faking? And if so, why? I began asking her a series of questions to try to determine whether she had really lost her memory. I also asked the office staff to page the school nurse and to try to reach her parents. Her responses to my questions were very odd. The office staff reached her father at work first, so I briefly explained the situation to him and then put Valerie on the phone with him in my office. I couldn't believe it. She acted as if she didn't know her dad! He was very concerned and asked me to keep her while he called their doctors. He called back shortly and told me that he had made an appointment for her with a neurologist at the local hospital and he would be there in 20 minutes to pick her up.

In the meantime, I received a call from her mother. She told me that this was all nonsense and that Valerie was faking it. She explained that Valerie wanted to go to a different middle school and was acting out because her parents wouldn't let her change schools. She said, "This is just an act. Ignore Valerie's behavior and send her back to class."

The school nurse arrived and examined Valerie. She came to a similar conclusion as Valerie's mother. We thought she was faking a case of amnesia but were concerned as to why. At this point, Valerie had taken the amnesia act very far. She was now calling me "Counselor Lady" and was complaining that she couldn't see while trying to read a book upside down. It took all my professionalism and strength not to break into laughter. I really did feel for Valerie, as I knew something was clearly upsetting her for her to put on such a stunning performance.

Her parents showed up and began to argue with each other over what should be done about this situation. The school nurse suggested taking Valerie to see her pediatrician. The parents finally agreed. When they left, the school nurse told me that she had seen this type of situation before and was confident that Valerie's doctor would know how to handle this case.

The next morning, Valerie showed up at school happy-go-lucky as usual. She acted as if nothing had happened the day before. I spoke to her mother, who filled in the rest of the story. As we suspected, the doctor had found nothing physically wrong with Valerie but did explain to her all uncomfortable procedures he would order for her to make sure nothing was wrong. She kept up the act until her bedtime. When her mom tucked her in that night, she told her very sternly that she knew what she was up to and wanted her to wake up the next morning and be back to herself. Sure enough, Valerie listened to her mom and was back to her old self the next morning. Her mom shared some of the stress their family was going through. Her parents had decided to get divorced, and Valerie wanted to change to the other local middle school, as that is where all of her friends had gone after elementary school. With the additional unrest of her parents' separating, being with her friends had become even more important to Valerie.

Valerie and I never discussed the amnesia episode openly, but she still had an interest in changing schools. The next school year she transferred to that school and reportedly was very happy. I would sometimes see Valerie at her new school, and she seemed to have adjusted easily. I never saw Valerie in my office again, and in my business, that's a good sign.

In this case, changing schools helped Valerie feel more secure, given the upheaval she was experiencing at home. This was a good reason to change schools. I am sure we could have worked out the transfer without her amnesia episode, but it goes to show how creative and dramatic middle-school students can be when they want something.

Changing classes or changing schools can be a good idea in certain situations. You just want to make sure that you don't make these changes as a way of running away from problems. It is important that we help our children learn to deal with the issues they face and find solutions that they can work through. Finding solutions and coping mechanisms is a great life skill that they will need as adults.

Chapter 9

Resources—where to get the help you need

As the saying goes, "It takes a village to raise a child." Yet in today's busy world, parents tend to go at it alone. Not a good idea.

Parenting is not an easy task, so don't be afraid to ask for help. Even if your child is sailing through the tween years easily, parents need support. So reach out and don't do it alone.

In times of need, first look to your circle of friends and neighbors. We all have friends, but you should think about who would be the best person to help with a specific issue. For instance, if your son is being teased at school and you're not sure what to do, don't bother asking a friend from work who doesn't have children or the PTA president whose kids are all over-achievers, outgoing and extremely popular. Ask a friend who may have older sons who were introverted during middle school. When asking for advice, be choosy about whom you turn to for what type of advice.

Family also can be a great resource even if it is just for support in what you are going through. In fact, in some cases, asking for support can be a wonderful way to bring families closer together when life keeps everyone busy and infrequently in touch. Don't be afraid to ask for help. There is no room for a big ego in parenting. No one is a parenting expert on every topic, but people who have been in your shoes before may be able to provide strength and practical advice during a tough time.

Issues at school

If you find that your child is having issues at school, I always recommend talking with the teachers first. Since they are on the front line with the kids every day, it is only fair to get their perspective on the issue so that you, as a parent, can get a clearer picture of the issue. Remember, there are two sides to every story and your child may have a different perspective on a specific issue than the teacher. My experience has been that teachers are very willing to help out and make accommodations for students when needed. So, always start there.

Then, if the issue continues, go to the principal. Don't ever hesitate to request a meeting with the principal of your child's school. Principals are busy people, as we all are, but they are ultimately responsible for children's education and well-being during the school day and should know if there is an issue going on within the school. Additionally, there is a good chance that if your child is having a specific issue, other children may be experiencing the same thing. So, talk to the principal.

Physical and mental well-being

When you have a baby and he seems sick or fussy and uncomfortable, the first thing you usually do is call your pediatrician. As children grow up, their bodies seem stronger and they can tell us if something is wrong, so we tend to rely on our pediatricians less and less.

Your pediatrician is an expert in both the physical and cognitive developments of children from birth to age 18. Don't underestimate the doctor's ability to provide insight into issues that may be occurring when your child is 10 to 13 years old. Many parents don't know this, but you can make an appointment with your pediatrician to discuss an issue privately before bringing your child in for an examination. Just ask, and your child's doctor will schedule either a phone or an in-person appointment with you to talk first. That way, you and the doctor can come up with a game plan to help your child without his feeling embarrassed or as if everyone is ganging up on him.

Your pediatrician may also be a great resource for finding help within your community. Doctors see a lot of families with a lot of different issues and therefore tend to be up to date on available resources in the community for a variety of issues. Don't hesitate to consult your pediatrician if your child is having difficulty in school, with friends or at home. The doctor may be able to help.

Google

It seems that we all turn to the Internet for everything these days. Well, that includes parenting advice. As you can imagine, there are a number of Websites that provide ideas, information and support systems for people raising children. Keep in mind that information you find on the Internet isn't always provided by experts in the field, so you have to rely on your own good judgment to sort through the useful and the useless. But there is a lot of good information out there, and there are definitely ways to find support if you don't have a resource in your local community.

Your instincts

The bottom line is that you know your child better than anyone else. If you are seeing behaviors changing and situations that don't seem right to you, then they probably need some attention. Rely on your gut instincts to get help when you feel you need it. Other people may try to dismiss or downplay your concerns, but if you feel strongly about something, follow your gut as you are probably on to something.

Stay connected

As part of my ongoing interest in helping parents of middle-school students, I have a Website and a quarterly newsletter that I am happy to share with you. Check them out, and I hope that you will find them helpful. Also, feel free to reach out to me with specific questions/issues/discussions, as I am happy to help in any way I can.

SurvivingMiddleSchoolForParents.com

About the author

I started my career in the marketing/advertising world, following in my dad's footsteps. When I finished my bachelor's degree all I wanted was a business suit and a feminine-looking brief case. I got both and then found a job in the computer industry, where I didn't need either. What I did need was a good sense of humor and willingness to work long hours. Luckily, I had both of those, too. After 10 years and much success, I realized that marketing computer hardware was not satisfying to me, and I found myself very tired. I decided I was too young to be so tired, so I took a leave of absence and spent the summer as a counselor of high school students on an educational trip abroad. I worked seven days a week, 24 hours a day, for an entire summer but have never felt so energized.

When I returned home, I realized that I had to change my career and began looking for my life's work. After a long search, I found it in school counseling. I entered graduate school focused on becoming a high school counselor. I wanted to help young people find their paths in life as I had just done. My master's program emphasized learning about group dynamics and family systems. The program also required working in various school settings. I took an internship in a middle school only because I had to serve a certain number of hours in with different age groups. My true passion at that time was to continue my work at the local high school. Well, once I worked in a middle school, I never went back.

Middle-school students fascinated me, as they are so young yet manage so much. It is an age where there are so many changes going on physically and emotionally that they often wear their feelings right on their sleeves. I learned so much from their honesty and childlike innocence while watching them work so hard to hide those qualities.

People used to say to me, "You must be crazy to want to work in a middle school. Kids are so awful during that age." I actually felt the exact opposite. Middle school is a wonderful age of opportunity. It offered me an opportunity to help teach these kids survival skills that not only will help them get through middle school but also will take them out into the world.

Middle school can be a crazy sort of place, but the kids are great and so are many dedicated staff members. While I was working, there were a number of occasions when I quietly would say to myself, "Wow, that one's going to make it into my book some day."

Well, that day has come. Enjoy.

CPSIA information can be obtained
at www.ICGtesting.com
Printed in the USA
FSOW02n1126250516
20789FS